The Wealth Creation Method

The Entrepreneur's Guide to Financial Freedom

Phil Calandra

The Wealth Creation Method
The Entrepreneur's Guide To Financial Freedom

Published by Reflek Publishing

The information provided in this book, *The Wealth Creation Method*, is for educational and informational purposes only. It is not intended to be, and should not be construed as, financial, investment, tax, or legal advice. The strategies, concepts, and examples discussed are general in nature and may not be suitable or applicable to your specific financial situation. While every effort has been made to ensure the accuracy of the information presented, this book is not a substitute for professional guidance tailored to your unique circumstances.

You are solely responsible for making your own financial decisions. Before implementing any strategies or making any financial, tax, or legal decisions, you should consult qualified professionals, including, but not limited to:

- A Certified Public Accountant (CPA) or tax advisor for guidance on your tax situation.
- A Licensed Attorney for legal advice, particularly in areas such as estate planning, business structuring, and asset protection.
- A Registered Investment Advisor (RIA) or other licensed financial professional for personalized investment guidance aligned with your goals and risk tolerance.

The examples, case studies, and hypothetical scenarios provided in this book illustrate concepts and strategies but do not guarantee or predict future outcomes. Past performance is not indicative of future results, and all investments carry risks, including the potential loss of principal.

The author, publisher, and any affiliates or associated entities disclaim any liability for any direct, indirect, consequential, or incidental loss or damage arising from the use of, or reliance on, the information contained in this book. By reading this book, you acknowledge and accept that you are solely responsible for the financial decisions you make.

The views expressed in this book are those of the author and do not necessarily reflect the views or positions of any regulatory body. No regulatory agency has reviewed or approved this book.

ISBN: 978-1-968164-07-2 (Paperback)

ISBN: 978-1-968164-08-9 (Ebook)

Dedication

To my wife, Trish—
Your unwavering love, patience, and belief in me are the foundation of every word I write. You are my greatest inspiration, and the success of our journey simply doesn't happen without you.

To my sons, Davis and Kyle—
You are the light of my life and the reason I strive to be better every day. May you always chase your dreams with courage and conviction.

To my mother, Joyce—
For your boundless encouragement and the strength you've instilled in me. Your support has carried me further than words can ever express.

To my grandfather, Col. Arnold Sokol—
My hero, my guiding star, and the embodiment of honor, courage, and dedication. Your legacy lives on in every step I take and every story I tell.

And to my future self, relax. You made it, and you lived life well!

Here's A Gift Before You Even Begin!

To say thanks for getting the book and investing in your financial future, here are some gifts to help you create wealth and freedom.

- The Wealth Creation Method Companion Workbook
- Your Wealth Freedom Number Calculator
- 12 Rapid Profit Drivers Manual
- The Wealthy Entrepreneur's Investment Playbook
- Profit Acceleration Simulator

Get your free gifts here:
https://truwealthadvisors.com/book-resources

Table of Contents

FOREWORD

THE WEALTH CREATION METHOD

Let me be real with you for a minute: I've spent way too many years watching talented, hardworking friends find ways to earn a ton of money—only to see them spend it just as fast. (Yup, guilty over here too!) They get caught on the hamster wheel, obsessing over top-line revenue and bragging about it, yet somehow, that money never translates into true wealth. They wake up one day wondering why they've worked so hard for so many years but have so little to show for it. Honestly, what's the point of all that effort if there's nothing to enjoy at the end of it all? Well, that's exactly what this book is here to change.

And yeah, I know if I came across yet another book promising "the secrets to creating wealth" or claiming to hold the "magic formula for getting rich," I'd probably roll my eyes too. Had I not personally known the author and called him a friend, I might have dismissed it outright. But I can tell you—this book is different. It isn't filled with fluff or empty promises. It's written by a man who's literally created insane sums of wealth—for himself and countless clients and entrepreneurs—by focusing on what actually works.

Now, I should give you a quick warning. If you're expecting some magic pill, some overnight shortcut that turns you into a millionaire by tomorrow, this isn't that kind of book. And if you're looking for "easy," well, prepare to be disappointed. But if you're ready for "simple"—simple to learn, simple to implement, and simple to make work—you're holding exactly what you need. And here's the best part: it's never too late. Phil's approach isn't about theories or pipe dreams. It's real-world, proven, and based on over two decades of navigating what most entrepreneurs never see coming: the rollercoaster of earning, expenses, paying yourself, and trying not to go broke in the process.

What really struck me when I read the transcript was how authentic and grounded Phil is. His advice? It's honest, practical, and honestly, relatable. He's been in the trenches—building businesses, consulting top brands, and trying to escape what he calls the revenue trap. That's why he *gets* you. He *is* you—an entrepreneur who's faced the same cycles of cash flow chaos, expenses, and the constant hustle. He understands the challenge of trying to grow a business while also trying to keep some semblance of personal wealth—and doing both without losing your mind.

And that's the secret sauce: Instead of being stuck in a cycle of earning more and still having less, Phil teaches you how to build a *system*. Step by step, brick by brick, transforming your business profits into your own personal ATM. Not just that—it also provides a clear blueprint for what to do with that cash once it's in your hand. That's what makes this approach so powerful.

Phil's whole philosophy is rooted in the idea that wealth isn't just a number or a status symbol. It's freedom. It's *time*. It's the *choice* to live life on your own terms—whether that's playing with your kids, traveling the globe, or simply doing what makes you happy. Because, let's face it—the best thing money can buy is choice.

And if you're not bought in yet, let me give you a quick sneak peek at some of the gold nuggets you'll discover inside:

- The Revenue Trap: You're raking in the dollars, but your personal net worth isn't budging. Why? Because most entrepreneurs pay too much in taxes. Phil shows you how to approach tax planning proactively—setting up your entities, timing your transactions, and documenting everything just right so Uncle Sam takes less and you keep more.
- The Wealth Transfer Protocol: Think of it as a high-tech pipeline—no more leaky buckets. The goal?

Consistency, automation, and making sure every dollar is working for *you*—24/7, even when you're sleeping.

- The Authority in Chaos: When your CPA, lawyer, and wealth manager aren't talking to each other, it's chaos. Phil advocates for a "Chief Wealth Officer"—someone who becomes your ecosystem's conductor, organizing all your advisors into a cohesive team. Because when they work together, they create harmony—and real results.

What I appreciate most about this book—and trust me, I've read a lot of financial and guru books in my years—is how no-nonsense and practical it is. This book doesn't just give ideas; it gives you tools, systems, and routines that you can implement today. And best of all, Phil doesn't sugarcoat the challenges—he acknowledges the hard truths, like how entrepreneurs are often their own worst enemies who sabotage their wealth with false beliefs, fragmented advice, and a mentality that wealth is an unachievable dream. But it's not. It's closer than you think, and turning the pages that you're about to consume is the best next step for you to take. I'm cheering you on.

Chris Harder
Founder, investor, and host of *The Chris Harder Show*

Preface

Why I Wrote This Book Now

Since I was eleven years old, when I faced suspension for selling cinnamon toothpicks on the school bus, entrepreneurship has been my calling. Since then, I've experienced every high and low this journey has to offer.

I began my professional entrepreneurial journey when I left a corporate consulting career immediately after September 11, 2001. I've built businesses from the ground up, celebrated hard-earned wins, and faced setbacks that pushed me to my limits. I've known the thrill of seeing a vision come to life, and I've felt the crushing weight of financial uncertainty when things didn't go as planned. Being a financial advisor during the Great Financial Crisis of 2008 was no fun, but it certainly taught me a great deal about running a business and managing personal finances.

Through it all, one truth has become clear: Entrepreneurship is a double-edged sword. On one hand, it offers the promise of freedom, fulfillment, and financial success. On the other, it can trap you in cycles of stress, instability, and constant hustle. I have personally and professionally experienced both sides of this dichotomy, which served as the inspiration for this book.

Over the years, I've worked with hundreds of entrepreneurs—some wildly successful, others struggling to find their footing. Despite their differences, I noticed a recurring pattern. Even those who managed profitable businesses frequently experienced financial hardship. They were generating revenue, managing teams, and achieving the kinds of milestones that others dream of. Yet when it came to personal wealth, they were stuck.

This realization wasn't just academic for me. It hit close to home. I've experienced this situation multiple times. I know how it feels to pour everything into your business, only to look at your personal finances and wonder where all that hard work went. In my early years as a business owner, I made the same mistakes I've seen so many others make. I reinvested everything into growth, deferred my wealth creation for "someday," and assumed that success in business would automatically lead to financial freedom.

It didn't.

The turning point for me came once I realized that business success and personal wealth are not the same thing. They follow entirely different rules; they are two different games, and without a system to bridge the gap, even the most profitable business can leave you financially insecure. That's when I began developing the Wealth Creation Method—a systematic approach to turning business success into lasting personal fortune.

This method wasn't just born from working with others. It was forged in my career and life. I have personally tested, refined, and lived every principle I share in these pages. This advice isn't theory or guesswork. It's the result of twenty-five years of real-world experience, both as an entrepreneur navigating the ups and downs of business ownership and as a guide helping others escape the revenue trap.

I wrote this book because the hidden crisis of financially unstable entrepreneurs can no longer be ignored. This crisis involves the lives, dreams, and futures of the people who are the backbone of our economy, not just money. Entrepreneurs drive innovation, create jobs, and shape industries. But too many of them are sacrificing their financial security in the process.

The old playbook of waiting for a big exit or deferring wealth-building is no longer viable. Now, in full disclosure, my wife Trish and I have experienced two business exits that allowed us to become financially work-optional. It can be done, and it will change your family's life.

Economic volatility, rising taxes, and market saturation have made it riskier than ever to rely on "someday." The new rules of wealth demand a different approach—one that prioritizes building personal financial security alongside business growth.

This book is your road map to financial freedom. It's a step-by-step guide to escaping the revenue trap and building a financial ecosystem that works for you. You'll learn how to convert business profits into personal wealth, reduce taxes, grow investments, and design a life of freedom and security. Most importantly, you'll discover how to create a system that makes your business serve your life—not the other way around.

If you've ever felt stuck, stressed, or unsure of how to turn your entrepreneurial success into lasting wealth, this book is for you. It's time to stop feeling broke, reclaim your freedom, and build the financial future you deserve.

Let's begin.

Introduction

The Revenue Trap

You work hard. You built a business from nothing. Your revenue grows every year. But something feels off. Despite the impressive numbers on your profit and loss statement, your personal bank account doesn't reflect your business success. This disconnect between business profit and personal wealth is what I call the revenue trap—and it catches almost every entrepreneur.

The revenue trap works like this: You start a business, work incredibly hard to make some money, reinvest most earnings back into growth, pay yourself just enough to maintain your lifestyle, and repeat this cycle year after year. The business gets bigger. Your stress level rises. Your time freedom decreases.

But your personal wealth? It barely budges. You are on a treadmill, moving in place like a hamster on an increasingly sophisticated wheel—running faster but not getting anywhere in terms of building lasting wealth outside your business.

We call this being a "treadmill entrepreneur." Perhaps you've discovered ways to accelerate the treadmill, increase revenue, and generate more profit, but be cautious—you might find yourself ensnared in a never-ending cycle.

I see this pattern with entrepreneurs making $300,000 a year and those making $3 million. The revenue number changes, but the trap remains the same. They work tirelessly to build a profitable business, yet their personal assets, investments, and financial security remain surprisingly minimal. The business serves as both their greatest asset and their greatest constraint, as they are unable to stop working because nearly all their "wealth" is invested in the business itself.

This trap is particularly dangerous because it often disguises itself as success. Your peers see your growing company, your impressive client list, and the trappings of entrepreneurial achievement. Nobody realizes that behind the successful business facade, you worry about having enough saved for retirement (which I view as a work-optional lifestyle), wonder how you'll fund your kids' college education, or stress about what would happen if your industry faced disruption. You've built a machine that generates revenue, and perhaps profit, but not one that automatically converts that profit into personal wealth.

Most entrepreneurs don't even realize they're on this treadmill to oblivion until they've been running their business for five to seven years. By then, they've often missed years of wealth-building opportunities. They wake up one day and realize they own a job, not an asset. Their business requires their constant attention to generate income, and without them, it might be worth very little to anyone else.

The worst part? Traditional financial advice doesn't solve this problem. Most financial advisors, CPAs, and business coaches don't understand the unique challenges entrepreneurs face when trying to convert business success into personal wealth. They provide fragmented advice, focusing on specific aspects but never addressing the overall picture.

Financial advisors talk about investments but don't understand the realities of your business cash flow. CPAs focus on accurately filing current-year tax returns without thinking about next year's tax reduction strategy, let alone building long-term wealth. Business coaches and even fractional CFOs push for growth and profit acceleration without explaining how to extract it for personal benefit. Each advisor functions independently, leaving it up to you as the founder, business owner, and entrepreneur to integrate these disparate strategies into a clear, cohesive plan.

By picking up this book, you've taken the first crucial step toward escaping the revenue trap. You've recognized that business profit and personal wealth are distinct entities with distinct regulations. You're ready to build the bridge between your business success and lasting financial freedom.

The Missing Bridge

Most entrepreneurs fail to bridge the crucial gap between business success and personal wealth because they don't know the gap exists. They assume that if they simply make more money in their business, personal wealth will naturally follow. This assumption costs them millions in lost wealth-building opportunities.

Think about the entrepreneurs you know. How many are working incredibly hard, running successful businesses, yet still worry about money? How many could walk away from their businesses tomorrow and maintain their current lifestyle indefinitely?

Very few. The missing bridge between business profit and personal wealth explains this paradox.

This bridge doesn't appear magically once your business reaches a certain revenue or threshold. I've worked with entrepreneurs generating $10 million in annual revenue who have less personal wealth than some of my clients who earn $500,000. The difference isn't in how much their businesses make—it's in whether they've systematically built and crossed this bridge.

Building this bridge requires that you understand a fundamental truth: Your business and your personal wealth are two separate games you play. These financial games serve different purposes, exhibit different growth patterns, and require different optimization strategies. Your business exists to generate profit through active operations. Your personal wealth exists to generate freedom through passive appreciation and income. These systems need to work together in one holistic financial ecosystem, but they function according to entirely different rules.

Most entrepreneurs make the mistake of focusing 95% of their financial attention on their business and only 5% on their personal wealth strategy. They believe that growing the business is the only wealth strategy they need. This imbalance explains why so many successful business owners reach their fifties and sixties with enormous revenue but surprisingly little accumulated wealth outside their business.

The missing bridge has three main components that we'll explore throughout this book. First, you need systematic cash flow engineering—strategies to efficiently and consistently move money from your business to your personal wealth vehicles. Second, you need tax integration—approaches that minimize tax impact across both business and personal finances rather than optimizing each separately. Third, you need asset structure. When combined correctly, investment vehicles, entity structures, and wealth protection mechanisms are essential components of a comprehensive financial strategy.

Without all three components working together, money leaks out of your financial ecosystem. You might be making good decisions for your business but bad ones for your personal wealth. Or you might be saving taxes in your business but creating tax problems in your personal finances. Or worst of all, you might be growing a business that has no clear path to converting that growth into personal assets you control.

The traditional financial services industry doesn't help with this bridge-building because it's not designed for entrepreneurs. Most financial advice assumes you have a steady paycheck, a predictable income, and a clear separation between your work and personal finances. None of these assumptions apply to founders and entrepreneurs, whose financial lives are far more complex and interconnected.

This missing bridge explains why two entrepreneurs with identical businesses can end up in entirely different financial positions after ten years. One builds and crosses the bridge systematically, continuously moving money from business profit to personal assets. The other focuses exclusively on growing the business, assuming wealth will take care of itself. A decade later, the first entrepreneur has both a valuable business and significant personal wealth. The second has only a business and remains trapped by its demands.

Throughout this book, you'll discover exactly how to build this bridge for your situation. You'll learn which wealth vehicles work best for different types of businesses, how to structure your cash flow for maximum wealth accumulation, and how to coordinate all your financial advisors around a single wealth-building strategy.

The Wealth Creation Method

The Wealth Creation Method forms the backbone of this entire book. It's a comprehensive three-part framework that successful entrepreneurs use to transform high income into generational wealth. This method isn't theoretical—it's a practical system that I have used myself. My business partner and wife, Trish, and I have refined it by working with hundreds of entrepreneurs who have successfully made the journey from business profit to personal wealth.

The three parts of this method function holistically and synchronously. They are:

1. **The Wealthy Entrepreneur's Flywheel:** Optimizing your business and accelerating profit
2. **The Tax Reduction Code:** Keeping more of what you earn through smart tax planning
3. **Your Personal Wealth Engine:** An entrepreneur-centric approach to asset accumulation

The first component of the Wealth Creation Method is business optimization. Most entrepreneurs think they've optimized their business when they maximize revenue.

That is a trap. True business optimization for wealth creation focuses on profit acceleration and involves structuring your business to transfer profit to your personal balance sheet. This means creating the right entity structure, compensation systems, profit distribution methods, and exit potential. A business optimized for wealth creation often looks different from one optimized merely for revenue growth.

If you study all successful business enterprises, you quickly find a pattern. The successful entrepreneur stays laser-focused on continuous, incremental growth in key areas. The winners look for hidden profit opportunities within the business, and their search does not necessarily mean increasing marketing and advertising spending. Financial strategies to explore include pricing strategies, upselling, referral/JV programs, and digital marketing.

When you focus on accelerating profit, growth happens rapidly, and your wealth-building flywheel becomes compelling. It is about achieving growth through strategic improvements and maximizing existing resources. You must identify profit acceleration opportunities, create a data-driven plan, and commit to becoming more efficient and profitable. At TruWealth Advisors, we use a tool (appropriately named) called Profit Acceleration Software to help create such a plan. The key to business optimization is profit. And profit is the domino that knocks down all the other dominoes.

Optimization also includes strategies like creating the ideal entity structure for wealth transfer, not just tax savings. It involves setting up systematic profit distributions that don't jeopardize business cash flow. It requires building business assets that have value beyond your personal involvement. Most importantly, it means designing your business model to generate the types of cash flow that convert most efficiently to personal wealth.

The second component of the Wealth Creation Method Framework is strategic tax planning and reduction. Taxes represent the single biggest expense for most successful entrepreneurs—often consuming 40% or more of their income when all taxes are combined. Yet most tax activity performed with your CPA or accountant focuses narrowly on reducing this year's business taxes without considering the long-term wealth impact. Strategic tax planning takes a different approach, looking at your entire financial ecosystem—business and personal—over a multiyear horizon.

This component includes strategies like tax-optimized business exits, income timing and characterization, entity structuring across your entire financial ecosystem, and strategic use of retirement vehicles and legal tax code deductions. The goal isn't just to reduce this year's tax bill but to minimize tax drag on your wealth-building over decades. The proactive engagement of tax planning and strategic tax reduction can amount to millions in additional wealth over an entrepreneurial career.

And the third component in the Wealth Creation Method Framework is the Personal Wealth Engine. This goes far beyond basic investing. Personal wealth-building involves creating assets outside your business that grow independently of your work efforts. The miracle of uninterrupted compound interest is the key that unlocks wealth accumulation. These assets eventually generate enough passive income to support your lifestyle without requiring your active involvement in the business. This component transforms you from a business owner dependent on your company for income into a true investor who controls diverse assets.

Personal wealth-building includes strategies for real estate investing tailored to busy entrepreneurs, business diversification through strategic acquisitions, private investment opportunities typically not available to the general public, and specialized asset allocation structures designed for business owners. It also involves wealth protection mechanisms that keep your assets secure regardless of what happens in your business or the broader economy.

When the three components of the Wealth Creation Method work together, something remarkable happens. Your business becomes a wealth-accumulating machine rather than just an income source. Money moves systematically from business profit to personal assets, which then grow and generate their returns. Over time, your personal wealth begins to outpace your business growth, creating true financial independence.

This three-part framework solves the fundamental problem most entrepreneurs face: having their wealth potential trapped inside their business. When you implement the Wealth Creation Method, the hard work you put into building a successful business translates directly into personal financial freedom.

Throughout this book, we'll dive deep into each component of the Wealth Creation Method. You'll learn strategies to optimize your business for wealth transfer, reduce your tax burden across your entire financial ecosystem, and build personal assets that grow independently of your work efforts. By the end, you'll have a complete road map for converting your business success into a lasting personal fortune.

The Wealth Creation Method isn't about getting rich quick. It's about systematically getting wealthy by harnessing your business's profit-generating power to build assets you control. This bridge, which most entrepreneurs never cross, is crucial in determining whether you will continue to work and achieve true financial freedom.

The integrated approach makes this method different. Most financial guidance and advice addresses either business finances or personal finances, but rarely both as a unified system. The Wealth Creation Method recognizes that for founders and entrepreneurs, business and personal finances are deeply interconnected. Success requires optimizing the entire ecosystem rather than individual parts.

This book will show you exactly how to implement each component of the Wealth Creation Method in your situation. You'll learn which strategies work best for different types of businesses, revenue levels, and personal goals. You'll discover how to coordinate all your financial advice-givers around this unified approach rather than letting them work in isolation. Most importantly, you'll develop the mindset shift required to think like a wealth builder rather than just a business owner.

The entrepreneurs who implement this method often see dramatic results within the first year—not just in their financial statements but also in their peace of mind. They stop worrying about being trapped in their businesses forever. They gain confidence about their financial future regardless of business fluctuations. They sleep better knowing they're building wealth that will outlast their working years.

By the end of this book, you will possess all the tools you'll need to overcome the revenue trap and achieve genuine financial independence that surpasses your business. You'll understand exactly how to transform your entrepreneurial success into lasting personal wealth. And you'll have a clear, actionable plan to make that transformation happen starting today.

Chapter 1
The Wealth Paradox

The High-Income, Low-Wealth Reality

You make good money. Your business brings in six, seven, or even eight figures. Your friends and family think you have it made. But there's a secret you don't share at dinner parties: Despite your impressive income, you don't feel wealthy at all.

This is the entrepreneur's wealth paradox—the strange gap between making lots of money and being wealthy. It's like having a bucket with holes in the bottom. You keep pouring water in, but the level never rises as high as it should. Your business income can make you rich, but it might not lead to true wealth.

I see this pattern every day. Entrepreneurs who earn $500,000 or even millions per year often have surprisingly little to show for it. They live in nice houses and drive nice cars, but their net worth—the real measure of wealth—lags far behind what their income would suggest. One client came to me earning over $1.2 million annually from his medical practice, yet he had less than $300,000 saved for work-optional retirement at age fifty-two. Another had built a $5 million company but couldn't take a month off because her personal finances would crumble without her regular draws from the business.

This gap between income and wealth isn't just bad luck or poor money habits. It's a structural problem that's built into how most entrepreneurs manage the relationship between their business and personal finances. The skills that make you successful at growing a business are entirely different from the skills needed to build personal wealth. Business growth requires reinvestment, risk-taking, and resources focused on capturing market opportunities. Personal wealth-building requires systematic extraction, protection, and patient, compound growth outside the business. These approaches often conflict with each other, creating the paradox of business success not automatically leading to personal wealth.

The numbers tell this story clearly. A recent study of business owners with revenues between $1 million and $10 million showed that 75% had less than one year's income saved outside their business.

Think about that. Three-quarters of successful entrepreneurs would face financial stress within a year if their business income stopped.

This isn't wealth. It's high-income dependency.

Why does this happen? This phenomenon occurs because most entrepreneurs invest all their resources into their businesses. And perhaps that is precisely what you should be doing. But do not fall asleep on your holistic wealth goals. These entrepreneurs believe that growing the business is the path to wealth. And while a bigger business might someday be worth more, that approach leaves them vulnerable today. Their personal balance sheets remain thin while their business balance sheets grow. Their financial future becomes completely tied to the fate of a single asset—their business.

This creates a dangerous trap. The bigger your business gets, the harder it becomes to extract yourself from it. You become essential to operations. Customers want to work directly with you. Employees need your guidance. The business demands more of your time, not less. Instead of the business becoming an asset that works for you, you become more deeply entrenched working for it.

Your business pays you well enough that you can't walk away, but it doesn't build wealth that would give you the freedom to choose whether to work or not. You end up with a high-paying job you created for yourself rather than true financial independence.

What's the worst part? This trap gets harder to escape with time. The longer you run your business without a systematic way to convert business success into personal wealth, the more entrenched the pattern becomes. Ten years pass, then twenty. Suddenly, you're approaching retirement age with a valuable business but little diversified wealth outside it. Your entire financial future hinges on selling the business for a premium price—an outcome that's far from guaranteed in most industries.

This high-income, low-wealth reality creates a particular kind of stress that's unique to successful founders. On the surface, everything looks great. You have the trappings of success. But privately, you worry about the future. You wonder if all your hard work will ever translate into lasting security. You question whether you'll ever reach the point where work becomes optional rather than financially necessary.

The False Beliefs Holding You Back

Behind every wealth paradox lies a set of beliefs that seem logical but block the path from revenue to wealth. These beliefs are particularly dangerous because they contain just enough truth to seem credible while leading you in exactly the wrong direction. Let's expose these wealth-blocking myths for what they are.

The first and most damaging belief is that business revenue growth automatically equals personal wealth growth. This seems so obvious that few entrepreneurs question it. If your business grows from $1 million to $5 million in revenue, surely your personal wealth should grow proportionally, right? But the data shows this rarely happens. In fact, more money creates more problems unless managed properly. Business growth often means more complexity, more employees, more overhead, and more stress—but not necessarily more transferable wealth for the owner. Growth that stays trapped in the business doesn't increase your personal net worth until you can extract that value.

Many entrepreneurs tend to measure their wealth based on their business revenue rather than their personal balance sheet. They'll proudly say, "We're a seven-figure business," while having less saved for a work-optional lifestyle (retirement) than many of their employees. Revenue is vanity, profit is sanity, but personal wealth is what provides freedom. Your business could generate millions while leaving you personally vulnerable if you haven't built the bridge between business success and personal assets.

The second false belief is that reinvesting everything back into the business is *always* the smartest move. Business gurus reinforce this myth, praising entrepreneurs who bet it all on their companies. While strategic reinvestment is essential for growth, the all-or-nothing approach creates serious wealth-building problems. It concentrates all your financial eggs in one basket. It delays wealth-building during your prime earning years when compound growth would be most powerful. And it often leads to lifestyle creep as the business grows, making it even harder to build wealth later.

A more balanced approach recognizes that both your business revenue and your personal wealth need regular investment to grow. The wealthiest entrepreneurs I know follow a simple rule: They pay themselves first, just like they pay their most important vendors. They treat personal wealth-building as a non-negotiable business expense rather than something that happens only if there's money left over.

The third wealth-blocking belief is that you'll cash out big someday when you sell your business. This exit fantasy keeps many entrepreneurs working for decades without building wealth outside their companies. They pour everything into growing business value, assuming they'll convert that value to cash in one big transaction down the road. However, the Exit Planning Institute (EPI) reports that fewer than 30% of businesses that enter the market make a sale.

Even successful exits often deliver less wealth than expected after taxes, transaction costs, and earn-out periods. I've seen entrepreneurs walk away with less than half the headline sale price after all deductions. And those who do manage a successful exit often find themselves unprepared for life afterward, both financially and emotionally. Building wealth alongside your business provides options, whether an exit happens or not. My wife and I lived this truth. Having exited two businesses, I assure you, it is not as simple as many believe.

The fourth false belief is that complex tax strategies alone will make you wealthy. Many entrepreneurs become obsessed with tax minimization, spending enormous energy on strategies to reduce their tax bill. While smart tax planning matters, focusing exclusively on paying less tax this year can harm long-term wealth-building. Some tax reduction strategies that look great on paper end up trapping capital in inefficient structures or creating future tax problems that outweigh the immediate savings. Kicking the can down the road is not always a winning strategy. For example, following typical traditional financial wisdom and maxing out your tax-deferred qualified plan for maximum tax write-offs may be the worst strategy for the founder or entrepreneur.

True wealth-building integrates tax planning with investment strategy, cash flow management, and risk protection. The goal isn't just to pay less tax—it's to keep more of what you make and grow it more effectively over time. Sometimes, paying a reasonable tax now unlocks much greater wealth-building opportunities than complex avoidance strategies.

The fifth and perhaps most insidious belief is that you'll focus on wealth-building "someday," when the business is more stable. This perpetual postponement keeps entrepreneurs stuck in wealth limbo for decades. There's always another growth opportunity, another market challenge, another reason to delay systematic wealth-building. Before you know it, you're fifty-five with a successful business but far less personal wealth than your income should have created.

The most financially successful business owners I've worked with started building wealth from day one, even if in small amounts. They recognized that wealth-building is a habit and a system, not an event that happens in the future. They understood that time in the market beats timing the market, especially when it comes to building assets outside your business.

The True Cost of Financial Fragmentation

Most entrepreneurs have a financial team that's not really a team at all. They have a CPA or accountant who handles preparing the tax returns once a year, a bookkeeper who manages the transactions in a software program, maybe a financial advisor who suggests investments, and perhaps a fractional CFO who looks only at business KPIs. Each of these professionals operates independently, striving to optimize their roles without considering the overall picture.

This fragmented approach to financial guidance is costing you a fortune in missed opportunities, unnecessary taxes, and wealth-building inefficiency.

Financial fragmentation creates three major wealth-draining problems. First, it leads to conflicting strategies that cancel each other out. Your CPA might recommend a certain business structure to save taxes, while your financial advisor suggests investment approaches that create tax problems the CPA never anticipated. Your fractional CFO might set up a cash flow forecast but never ask about your personal cash flow objectives. Without coordination, these professionals often work at cross-purposes, each undoing the benefits the others created.

I recently worked with a business owner who had implemented tax strategies his CPA suggested that were saving about $30,000 annually in business taxes. Sounds wonderful, right? But those same strategies were blocking him from contributing to work-optional retirement accounts and forcing him to take income in ways that created over $45,000 in additional personal taxes. The business tax savings were causing a net loss when I looked at his entire financial picture. No single advisor had the complete view needed to see this problem.

Here is another example: A fractional CFO had built a great cash flow forecast, implemented a few cost-cutting measures, and identified a chart of accounts. But they failed to recognize a significant tax-free income solution using the Augusta Rule (IRC Sec. 280A).

The second cost of fragmentation is missed connection opportunities between business and personal finances. Your business creates unique wealth-building opportunities that most financial advisors don't understand because they work primarily with employees, not business owners and entrepreneurs. Your personal financial situation creates business structuring possibilities that most business consultants never consider because they focus only on the company, not your broader wealth goals.

These missed connections can be enormously expensive. One client had been contributing to a traditional 401(k) for years on his financial advisor's recommendation while running a successful consulting business. Neither his CPA nor his advisor had mentioned that with his business structure and income level, he could have been using a different retirement vehicle that would have allowed nearly three times the annual contribution. This oversight cost him over $720,000 in lost retirement savings over eight years.

Third. The most costly aspect of fragmentation is the opportunity cost resulting from delayed action. When your financial guidance and advice come from multiple uncoordinated sources, decision-making becomes complicated and slow. You get conflicting recommendations, which leads to analysis paralysis. You wait for a consensus that never comes, and you become the bottleneck because of confusion. Meanwhile, wealth-building opportunities pass by unused. Investment positions remain untaken. Tax strategies go unimplemented until it's too late to capture their full benefit.

This delay cost is particularly severe for entrepreneurs because their financial situation changes rapidly as their business evolves. The right wealth-building strategy last year might be entirely wrong this year as your income, business structure, and opportunities shift. Without a coordinated team that can move quickly, you're perpetually implementing strategies that would have been perfect for your situation twelve to twenty-four months ago but may be suboptimal now.

Financial fragmentation also creates enormous stress. You become your financial team's reluctant quarterback, trying to coordinate advisors who speak different professional languages and have different priorities. You spend valuable time in meetings, explaining what another advisor recommended, trying to reconcile conflicting advice, and making decisions you don't feel fully qualified to make. The toll of this cognitive and emotional burden extends far beyond the direct financial costs.

The wealthiest entrepreneurs solve this problem by implementing what I call "financial integration." They either find advisors who understand both business and personal finances as an integrated system or create a coordinated team with a clear hierarchy and communication structure.

At TruWealth Advisors, we call this a chief wealth officer. They ensure that everyone working on their finances shares information regularly and works toward common goals rather than optimizing in isolation.

This integrated approach typically saves six or seven figures over an entrepreneurial career through more efficient tax strategies, better investment opportunities, reduced fees, and faster implementation of wealth-building systems. More importantly, it dramatically reduces financial stress by creating clarity and confidence about your wealth strategy's overall direction.

Your Wealth Creation Scorecard

Wealth Creation Scorecard

The Wealth Creation Scorecard is a comprehensive self-assessment tool designed to help you evaluate the alignment and effectiveness of your personal and business financial systems. The scorecard provides a structured framework with twenty targeted questions that assess critical aspects of wealth-building, financial organization, and strategic financial independence.

Each question encourages you to rate your level of agreement on a scale of 1 to 5, ranging from "1 - Strongly Disagree" to "5 - Strongly Agree." The total score offers insights into your current financial position, highlighting areas of strength and those needing improvement.

The questions focus on key wealth-building principles, including

- Tracking personal wealth and net worth trends
- Coordinating with financial advisors, like CPAs and wealth managers
- Establishing proactive tax strategies and leveraging entity structures
- Building systems for cash flow management, profit extraction, and personal wealth conversion
- Planning for a work-optional lifestyle and financial continuity in case of absence
- Creating a coordinated financial plan that encompasses business continuity, tax efficiency, and estate planning

The scorecard also includes a scoring system that categorizes you into one of five performance tiers:

1. **Critical Misalignment (0–20):** Financial systems are dangerously out of sync, leading to inefficiencies, tax overpayments, and wealth leakage.
2. **Fragmented and at Risk (21–40):** Some systems are in place, but they are disconnected, causing stress and inefficiencies.

3. **Functional but Not Free (41–60):** Systems are solid but overly reliant on the business owner, limiting financial freedom.
4. **Stable but Not Scalable (61–80):** A strong foundation exists, but further optimization is needed to scale wealth without scaling stress.
5. **Work-Optional Wealth Architect (81–100):** The business is a fully functional wealth engine, allowing for autonomy, legacy planning, and financial independence.

The tool concludes with personalized recommendations that are based on your score and aimed at addressing inefficiencies, reducing risk, and optimizing systems for greater financial alignment. The scorecard's ultimate goal is to guide you toward a work-optional lifestyle, where your business serves as a reliable engine for personal wealth and legacy creation.

This framework provides a practical and actionable road map that you can use to transition from financial misalignment to complete autonomy, empowering you to focus on long-term wealth-building and financial freedom.

How much wealth should your business be creating for you? Most entrepreneurs have no clear answer to this question. They know they should be building more wealth, but they have no benchmark for what's possible given their business situation. Without this benchmark, it's impossible to know if you're on track or falling dangerously behind in your wealth-building journey.

The Wealth Creation Scorecard provides this crucial benchmark by calculating the gap between your current financial reality and what's possible based on your business success. This isn't about comparing yourself to other entrepreneurs or some arbitrary standard. It's about measuring your personal wealth-building efficiency based on your own business performance.

Chapter 1 Recap: Breaking Free from the Revenue Trap

We've uncovered the fundamental paradox that keeps successful entrepreneurs working hard but feeling financially insecure. You now understand that business profit and personal wealth are separate games requiring different strategies. Let's recap the key insights from this chapter and outline your first action steps toward breaking free from the revenue trap.

Key Insights

The Entrepreneur's Wealth Paradox

- Business success doesn't automatically translate to personal financial security.
- True wealth comes from assets that grow and generate income without requiring your active involvement.

The High-Income, Low-Wealth Trap

- Many entrepreneurs generate impressive revenue but lack significant personal wealth outside their business.
- This creates a dangerous dependency on your business, tying your financial security to your constant involvement.

False Wealth-Building Beliefs

- Myth #1: Business growth automatically leads to personal wealth.
- Myth #2: Reinvesting everything into the business is the best strategy.
- Myth #3: "Someday" you'll cash out big and solve everything.
- Myth #4: Minimizing taxes is more important than maximizing long-term wealth.
- Myth #5: Postponing wealth-building for a better future is a safe bet.

The Cost of Financial Fragmentation

- Multiple advisors (CPA, bookkeeper, CFO, financial planner, attorney, etc.) often work in silos, creating conflicts and inefficiencies.
- Fragmentation leads to missed opportunities, confusion, and poor implementation.
- A Chief Wealth Officer or a better-integrated system could optimize your financial strategy.

The Wealth Creation Scorecard

- A tool to measure the gap between your current financial state and what's possible.
- Provides benchmarks to track progress as new strategies are implemented.

Action Steps

1. Complete the Wealth Creation Scorecard

- Access the online tool (link provided in the book).
- Answer honestly—this baseline assessment is critical to identifying gaps in your wealth-building potential.
- Understand your current performance (many entrepreneurs are shocked to find they operate at only 10%-20% of their potential).

2. Identify Wealth-Blocking Beliefs

- Review the false beliefs outlined in this chapter:

    - Are you reinvesting everything without building personal wealth?
    - Are you delaying wealth-building strategies for the future?
    - Are you relying on a "big payday" exit that may never materialize?
  - Write down which beliefs resonate most with your decisions.
  - Acknowledge how these beliefs have influenced your financial strategy so far.

3. Map Your Financial Ecosystem

  - Create a list of all your current financial advisors (CPA, bookkeeper, financial advisor, attorney, insurance agent, etc.).
  - Evaluate their level of communication with each other:
    - Are they aligned on your financial goals?
    - Is anyone overseeing your entire financial picture?
  - Identify gaps, overlaps, or inefficiencies in how advice is being given and implemented.

4. Reflect on Your Financial Dependency

  - Ask yourself:
    - If you stopped working tomorrow, how long could your wealth sustain you?
    - Are your current assets independent of your business's performance?

Key Takeaways for Transformation

- Focus on Integration: Financial success requires a cohesive strategy, not fragmented advice.
- Shift Your Mindset: True wealth-building starts by addressing limiting beliefs and prioritizing long-term strategies over short-term wins.
- Measure & Optimize: Use tools like the Wealth Creation Scorecard to track your progress and identify areas for improvement.

Next Steps in the Book

- Learn how to optimize your business structure for wealth extraction without harming growth.
- Discover tax strategies that reduce drag across your financial ecosystem.
- Build assets that grow independently of your efforts, creating lasting financial independence.

Chapter 2

The Wealthy Entrepreneur's Flywheel

Your Business as Your Wealth Generator

Your business is not just a way to make a living. It's a way to make your legacy. It's the most powerful wealth-building tool you'll ever have. Most entrepreneurs miss this critical point. They run their businesses focused only on growth, sales, and solutions to day-to-day problems. They never step back to see the bigger picture—that their business should be designed to be a wealth engine that powers their entire financial lives.

Think about it this way. A regular employee might save 10% to 15% of their income if they're disciplined. But as a business owner, you can potentially extract 30% to 40%

of your business profits to build personal wealth while still growing your business. This wealth-building advantage is enormous, but only if you structure your business to capture it.

The problem is that most business owners accidentally build businesses that trap wealth instead of transferring it. They create companies that demand constant reinvestment, personal time, and attention. Their businesses become like hungry teenage boys who constantly need feeding, never quite growing up to support the parents who raised them. The business makes money, but that money stays stuck, spinning in a perpetual cycle of growth and operations rather than building your personal fortune.

I worked with a marketing agency owner who had built a $3 million business over twelve years. On paper, it looked impressive. But when we analyzed his personal finances, he had less than $200,000 in assets outside the business despite earning high six figures for over a decade. His business was successful, but it wasn't functioning as a wealth flywheel. It was more like a high-paying job he had created for himself—one with all the stress of ownership but without the long-term wealth benefits.

You need to make the critical mindset shift from seeing yourself as a business owner to becoming a wealthy entrepreneur. A business owner focuses on making the business bigger and more profitable. A wealthy entrepreneur designs the business to efficiently create personal wealth. This subtle difference in perspective changes everything about how you structure, operate, and extract value from your company.

Wealthy entrepreneurs understand that business metrics, like revenue and profit, are valuable only if they can be converted into personal wealth. They measure success not just by the size of their company but by how effectively their business builds their net worth outside the business. They ask different questions: "How much wealth is my business creating for me personally?" instead of just "How much profit is my business generating?"

This shift requires thinking about your business as part of an integrated wealth system rather than your entire financial identity. Your business should be the flywheel that powers wealth creation, but the wealth also needs to exist outside the business to be secure. Otherwise, you risk creating a situation where your entire financial future hinges on the sustained success of a single asset—your company.

The Wealthy Entrepreneur's Flywheel works like this: Your business generates profit. You systematically extract a portion of that profit and transfer it to personal wealth vehicles. These vehicles grow independently of your business, creating diversified assets you control. As these assets grow, they provide financial security that allows you to make better business decisions without fear. Better decisions lead to more business profit, which allows more wealth extraction. This cycle accelerates over time, building both business value and personal wealth simultaneously. This is precisely why the flywheel is such a valuable tool.

Unfortunately, many founders fall short in creating their business flywheel. They don't generate and accelerate profit in their enterprise. In this context, business optimization and profit acceleration are synonymous. Think of profit acceleration as the power source for your business flywheel. The faster and larger you can make your flywheel, the faster you will become a wealthy entrepreneur.

Take a strategic approach to increase profitability—fast. Remember, success loves speed. This will likely involve identifying key areas where enhancements or optimizations can lead to significant improvements in financial performance. The primary aim is to achieve quicker and more substantial growth in profits by focusing on strategies that can yield immediate results. Sometimes, businesses may overlook small changes that can lead to significant increases in profit margins. Accelerating profit is about identifying these areas and implementing actionable steps that can be monitored and measured for their impact.

Start effective profit acceleration by thoroughly analyzing your current operations. This may involve looking at sales processes, marketing efforts, pricing strategies, and cost structures to uncover areas that can be improved. For instance, enhancing customer acquisition and retention strategies can lead to increased sales, while renegotiating supplier contracts might reduce costs and improve margins.

The next step involves setting clear objectives based on this analysis, with a focus on KPIs that can track progress. You should be using data analytics, customer feedback, and internal team member insight as tools to refine your business flywheel. Another vital aspect of profit acceleration is streamlining operations to improve efficiency. Identifying bottlenecks and implementing solutions can reduce costs, increase profit, and begin moving you toward wealth creation.

It is common for business leaders to stress over KPI data. This does not need to be complex. To transform your business into a true wealth creator, you need to optimize what I call the critical four. These four numbers determine how effectively your business can build personal wealth. They are revenue, gross profit, net profit, and cash flow. Most entrepreneurs focus only on revenue, but the other three metrics are more important for wealth creation. Let's explore each one and how to optimize it specifically for wealth-building.

The Critical Four: Revenue

Revenue gets all the attention. Entrepreneurs brag about hitting seven figures. Business magazines celebrate the fastest-growing companies. Everyone seems obsessed with top-line growth. But revenue alone means nothing for wealth creation. What matters is profitable revenue that you can efficiently convert to personal wealth. This requires a completely different approach to revenue optimization than what most business gurus teach.

The first principle of revenue optimization for wealth creation is client selection. Not all revenue is created equal. Some clients demand enormous resources and constant attention. They also create operational complexity that eats into profits. Others pay promptly, require minimal hand-holding, and fit perfectly into your existing operations. Wealthy entrepreneurs ruthlessly focus on the second category.

I worked with a consultant who cut his client roster from twenty-five to twelve, deliberately eliminating his highest-maintenance clients, even though some were big spenders. His revenue dropped by 15%, but his profit increased by 40%. And his personal stress level plummeted. More importantly, he freed up time to build wealth-generating assets outside his business. His company became a more efficient wealth flywheel because it was serving fewer, better clients.

The second principle is pricing psychology. Most entrepreneurs underprice their products or services because they focus on competition rather than value. They ask, "What does everyone else charge?" instead of "What is the true value we deliver?" This mindset keeps revenue artificially low and makes wealth creation much harder.

Wealthy entrepreneurs take a different approach. They quantify the value their solutions provide to clients, then price accordingly. They communicate this value clearly and confidently. They aren't afraid to be the premium option in their market because they understand that price is often a proxy for quality in clients' minds. This approach not only increases revenue but also attracts clients who appreciate value and cause fewer operational headaches.

One business owner I worked with doubled his prices after we calculated that his service saved clients an average of fifteen times what he charged. He lost some price-sensitive clients but replaced them with higher-quality ones who needed less support. His revenue increased by 70% while his work hours decreased. Most importantly, his business began generating enough profit to fund significant wealth-building outside the company.

The third principle is optimization. Many businesses create too many offers in an effort to please everyone. This complexity kills profitability and makes wealth extraction nearly impossible. Wealthy entrepreneurs do the opposite—they simplify their offers and focus on the most profitable core products or services.

This often means eliminating offers that clients occasionally request but that don't leverage your core strengths. It means saying no to projects that would require building new capabilities. It means standardizing your delivery process so it becomes more efficient over time. Each of these decisions might seem to limit revenue in the short term, but they dramatically increase the profit you can extract for wealth-building.

A software company owner I advised reduced his product line from seven different solutions to just two. His team initially worried about lost revenue, but something intriguing happened. With fewer products to support, they dramatically improved their core offerings. Marketing became more focused. Sales conversations simplified. Revenue increased by 35% within six months, while development costs dropped significantly. The business became a much more efficient wealth-building flywheel.

The fourth principle is leverage. Wealthy entrepreneurs structure their revenue streams to require less of their personal time and fewer resources per dollar earned. They build systems that allow the business to generate revenue without their constant involvement. This might mean creating digital products, implementing subscription models, building recurring revenue streams, or developing intellectual property that generates licensing income.

One business coach shifted from one-on-one consulting to group programs delivered through a combination of recorded content and live Q&A sessions. His hourly rate effectively tripled, and he reduced his working hours by 40%. The business became more scalable and less dependent on his personal time. Most importantly, he gained the freedom to focus on wealth-building activities outside his business while his revenue increased.

Revenue optimization for wealth creation often looks very different from traditional growth strategies. Occasionally, it means growing more slowly but more profitably. Occasionally, it means making less revenue but keeping more of what you make. Always, it means designing your business to transfer maximum value to your personal balance sheet rather than just creating an impressive top-line number.

The Critical Four: Gross Profit

Gross profit—the money left after paying for the direct costs of delivering your product or service—is the lifeblood of wealth creation. While revenue matters, gross profit determines how much money is available to either reinvest in growth or extract for personal wealth-building. Most entrepreneurs focus on increasing revenue without paying enough attention to maximizing the gross profit percentage, which limits their wealth-building potential.

The first strategy for gross profit maximization is cost structure analysis. This means taking a hard look at every direct cost associated with delivering your product or service. Most businesses accept their cost structure as fixed, but wealthy entrepreneurs question every expense and look for creative ways to reduce costs without sacrificing quality.

A manufacturing business I worked with conducted a detailed analysis of their materials costs and found they were using premium components in areas where customers couldn't tell the difference. By selectively substituting less expensive materials in noncritical areas, they increased their gross profit margin from 42% to 58% without any negative impact on product quality or customer satisfaction. This single change added over $300,000 annually to their bottom line, much of which the owner directed toward personal wealth-building.

The second strategy is strategic outsourcing. Many entrepreneurs try to do everything in-house, believing it saves money. But wealth entrepreneurs recognize that specialists can often perform certain functions more efficiently. They identify which parts of their delivery process are core to their value proposition and which ones others could handle at a lower cost.

One professional services firm outsourced their initial client research work to specialized contractors who could complete it in half the time it took their internal team. This reduced their delivery costs by 30% while improving quality. The firm maintained control of the strategy and client relationship—the parts clients valued—while outsourcing the time-intensive research that drained their margins. Their gross profit increased dramatically, creating more funds for the owner to extract for personal wealth-building.

The third strategy is technology leverage. Wealthy entrepreneurs constantly look for ways to use technology to reduce delivery costs and increase margins. This doesn't mean replacing human judgment with automation, but rather using technology to handle repetitive tasks so humans can focus on high-value work.

A financial advisory firm implemented software that automated their basic client reporting and portfolio rebalancing functions. This technology investment cost $50,000 up front but saved over $200,000 annually in staff time while improving accuracy. Their gross profit margin increased from 65% to 78%, creating substantial additional profit that the owner could direct toward personal wealth-building rather than reinvesting in the business.

The fourth strategy is delivery process optimization. Most businesses deliver their products or services the same way for years without questioning whether it's the most efficient approach. Wealthy entrepreneurs regularly analyze their delivery process to eliminate waste, reduce steps, and increase efficiency without compromising quality.

One consulting company mapped out their entire client delivery process and discovered they were spending an enormous amount of time creating custom reports for each client. By developing a standardized reporting framework with modular components that could be customized quickly, they reduced report creation time by 75% while improving client satisfaction. Their gross profit margin increased from 60% to 72%, creating additional profit that could be extracted for personal wealth-building.

The fifth strategy is pricing model innovation. Conventional pricing models frequently fail to maximize profits. Wealthy entrepreneurs experiment with different approaches, like value-based pricing, outcome-based fees, or tiered service levels to capture more of the value they create for clients.

A marketing agency shifted from hourly billing to fixed project fees based on the expected business impact of each campaign. For projects with measurable ROI, they added a performance component to their fees. This change increased their average project value by 40%, while clients appreciated the aligned incentives. Their gross profit margin jumped from 55% to 68%, creating substantial additional profit that the owner could direct toward building personal wealth.

Gross profit maximization requires constant vigilance and creativity. Markets change, costs shift, and new opportunities emerge. Wealthy entrepreneurs review their gross profit margins monthly and immediately address any downward trends. They recognize that even small improvements in gross profit percentage can dramatically increase the funds available for personal wealth-building over time.

The Critical Four: Net Profit and Cash

Net profit—what remains after all business expenses are paid—is what you can potentially extract to build personal wealth. But there's often a dangerous gap between paper profit and cash available for wealth-building. This is why wealthy entrepreneurs focus on engineering both net profit and cash flow simultaneously. They design their businesses not only to show profit on financial statements but also to generate cash they can transfer to personal wealth vehicles.

The first principle of net profit engineering is overhead optimization. Most businesses accumulate unnecessary overhead expenses over time—subscriptions no one uses, office space that's too large, staff positions that could be part-time, and perks that don't improve productivity. Wealth entrepreneurs regularly audit these expenses with a simple question: "Does this expense directly contribute to serving clients or generating revenue?"

I collaborated with a service business owner who undertook a zero-based budget exercise, scrutinizing each overhead expense as if he were initiating the business from the beginning. He discovered that his company was spending over $12,000 monthly on tools, subscriptions, and services that provided minimal value. By eliminating these expenses, he increased his annual net profit by nearly $150,000 without affecting revenue or client satisfaction. That's $150,000 more he could potentially extract for personal wealth-building.

The second principle is tax structure optimization. While we'll cover tax strategies in depth later in the book, it's important to recognize that business entity structure and tax planning directly impact how much profit remains available for wealth extraction. Wealthy entrepreneurs work with tax professionals who understand both business and personal finances to create integrated strategies that minimize total tax burden.

A business owner switched from an S corporation to a carefully structured C corporation with an additional LLC for certain operations. This reorganization reduced his combined business and personal taxes by over $70,000 annually while providing better asset protection. The tax savings went directly into his personal investment accounts, accelerating his wealth-building without requiring any change in business operations.

The third principle is the cash acceleration framework. It tackles the crucial discrepancy between profit and cash flow, a challenge that many entrepreneurs encounter. You might show a profit on paper but still lack cash because it's tied up in inventory, accounts receivable, or prepaid expenses. Wealthy entrepreneurs implement strategies to convert profit to cash faster.

These strategies include tightening payment terms with clients, offering discounts for prepayment, requiring deposits for work, implementing late fees, automating collections, negotiating extended terms with vendors, and minimizing inventory. Each approach helps close the gap between when you earn profit on paper and when you have cash available for wealth-building.

The fourth principle is capital efficiency. Many businesses tie up too much capital in equipment, facilities, or other assets that don't directly generate revenue. Wealthy entrepreneurs question every major capital expenditure and seek alternatives, like leasing, sharing, outsourcing, or using technology to reduce capital requirements.

A service business was planning to purchase a $175,000 piece of specialized equipment they used occasionally. Instead, they found a partner company with excess capacity that would provide the same service at a reasonable cost. This arrangement freed up $175,000 in capital that would have been tied up in equipment, allowing the owner to invest that money in income-producing assets outside the business. The small ongoing expense for the outsourced service was far less than the wealth-building opportunity cost of the capital expenditure.

The fifth principle is strategic profit allocation. Many entrepreneurs reinvest profits haphazardly, responding to whatever seems urgent at the moment. Wealthy entrepreneurs instead create a formal profit allocation system that prioritizes personal wealth extraction. They might use a framework like the profit-first method, which allocates a percentage of revenue to different accounts, including one for owner wealth-building.

One business owner implemented a modified profit-first system where 15% of all revenue automatically went into a separate account designated for his personal wealth-building. With this simple change, wealth extraction happened systematically rather than only when there happened to be extra" money left over. Over three years, this approach allowed him to build over $400,000 in investments outside his business while still funding necessary business growth.

Net profit and cash flow engineering require discipline and systems. Wealthy entrepreneurs don't leave these critical metrics to chance. They design their businesses to generate cash that can be extracted and moved to personal wealth vehicles. They recognize that a business that shows high profits on paper but never generates cash for the owner is not a true wealth engine.

Chapter 2 Recap: Optimizing Your Business for Wealth Creation

Your business can be the most powerful wealth-building tool you'll ever have, but only if you optimize it specifically for wealth creation. Throughout this chapter, we've explored how to transform your business from a mere income source into a true wealth engine by focusing on profit acceleration and what I call the critical four metrics: revenue, gross profit, net profit, and cash flow.

Key Insights

Shift from Business Owner to Wealthy Entrepreneur

- Measure success by personal net worth growth, not just business growth.
- Design your business to transfer value to your personal balance sheet, not trap wealth inside the company.

The Critical Four Metrics

- **Revenue**: Optimize income without increasing complexity or time demands.
- **Gross Profit**: Improve margins through cost analysis, outsourcing, and process optimization.
- **Net Profit**: Convert gross profit into extractable funds through overhead reduction, tax planning, and profit allocation.
- **Cash Flow**: Ensure cash is available for wealth-building by managing receivables, inventory, and capital efficiently.

The Wealthy Entrepreneur's Flywheel

- Better revenue → Higher gross profit → Greater net profit → Optimized cash flow → Extractable wealth for personal assets.
- This cycle transforms your business into a true wealth-generation engine.

Action Steps

1. Measure Your Current Metrics

- Calculate your:
  - Gross profit percentage.
  - Net profit percentage.
  - Gap between paper profit and extractable cash.
- Use these figures as a baseline for improvement.

2. Identify Your Weakest Metric

- Is your **revenue model** too time-intensive?
- Are your **gross profit margins** below industry benchmarks?
- Is **overhead** consuming too much profit?
- Is cash tied up in **receivables or inventory**?
- Pinpoint your weakest area to focus your initial efforts.

3. Implement One Optimization Strategy

- For Revenue:
  - Restructure your client mix to focus on profitable, low-demand customers.
  - Adjust pricing based on value delivered, not market averages.
- For Gross Profit:
  - Analyze costs and reduce inefficiencies.
  - Optimize your delivery process or leverage technology.
- For Net Profit or Cash Flow:

   - Reduce unnecessary overhead.
   - Use the cash acceleration framework to free up tied capital.

4. Track Metrics Monthly

   - Monitor all four metrics consistently—not just quarterly.
   - Use monthly tracking to identify issues and make adjustments immediately.
   - Create accountability and ensure wealth-building stays a priority.

Key Takeaways for Transformation

- **Leverage Your Business as a Wealth Engine**: Focus on systematically extracting value for personal wealth while maintaining growth.
- **Maximize Efficiency**: Small improvements in margins and processes can yield significant long-term gains.
- **Track and Adapt**: Consistent monitoring keeps your business aligned with your personal wealth goals.

Next Steps in the Book

- Learn how to minimize tax drag while optimizing cash flow.
- Explore strategies for systematically extracting and reinvesting wealth outside your business.
- Build a business structure that supports long-term wealth creation and financial independence.

Chapter 3

The Wealth Transfer Protocol

The Missing Link Between Business and Personal Wealth

You work hard in your business. You make good profits. But somehow, that money never seems to find its way into your personal wealth. This gap—the missing link between business success and personal fortune—keeps most entrepreneurs trapped in a cycle of making money but never feeling wealthy. It's like owning a gold mine that produces tons of gold, but you have no way to transport that gold from the mine to your home.

This missing link is what I call the Wealth Transfer Protocol—a systematic process for moving money from your business to wealth-building assets you personally control. Once you have accelerated profit and optimized your business's flywheel, this is critical. Without this protocol, your business becomes a bucket with holes. Money flows in through your hard work and smart decisions, but it leaks out through taxes, unnecessary expenses, and poor cash flow management before it can build your personal wealth.

The harsh truth is that most entrepreneurs never develop this protocol. They focus all their energy on growing their business, assuming that wealth will somehow take care of itself. They might have a vague plan to withdraw money when the business becomes more stable or to extract cash when they eventually sell the company. But these are not strategies. They're hopes. And hope is not a wealth-building plan.

I recently worked with Sarah, who owns a marketing agency that makes $1.8 million in annual revenue. On paper, her business looked fantastic—20% profit margins, a growing client list, and a talented team. But when we looked at her personal finances, the picture changed dramatically. Despite running this successful business for seven years, she had less than $100,000 in personal investments outside her company. Her business was making money, but she wasn't building wealth.

The problem wasn't that Sarah's business wasn't profitable enough. The problem was that she had no systematic way to transfer that profit into personal wealth. Money would pile up in the business bank account and then get reinvested in new projects or used for unnecessary expenses, or it would sit idle, earning minimal interest. Without a Wealth Transfer Protocol, her business success wasn't translating into personal financial security.

This missing link creates three major problems for entrepreneurs. First, it leads to wealth concentration risk—having too much of your net worth tied up in a single asset (your business). Your entire financial life is at risk if your industry experiences disruption, your business encounters difficult times, or the economy falters. Which does happen (i.e., The Great Financial Crisis of 2008 and COVID-19).

Second, it creates an unhealthy dependency that prevents you from stepping back from your business, as your financial survival relies on your constant involvement.

Third, it prevents the power of compound growth from working on your behalf, as money that could be growing in outside investments remains trapped in your business.

The Wealth Transfer Protocol solves these problems by creating a reliable bridge between your business finances and personal finances. It guarantees that a portion of every dollar your business earns systematically flows to assets you control outside the business—assets that grow even when you're not working, aren't tied to the fate of your company, and create true financial independence over time.

This protocol isn't just about taking owner distributions or paying yourself a salary. Those are components, but the complete protocol is much more comprehensive. It's a systematic approach that includes entity structuring, compensation planning, tax optimization, profit distribution systems, and personal investment strategies, all working together. When properly implemented, it creates an automatic wealth-building machine that requires minimal ongoing effort to maintain.

The entrepreneurs who implement this protocol see dramatically different results compared to those who don't. One client with a $5 million service business implemented the protocol five years ago. Today, he has over $2.7 million in personal investments outside his company—more than most business owners with companies twice his size. Another client with a smaller $800,000 business has built over $600,000 in outside investments in just three years using these same strategies. The protocol works regardless of business size because it's about systematic wealth transfer, not just business growth.

Designing Your Profit Distribution Strategy

The core of your **Wealth Transfer Protocol** is your **profit distribution strategy**—a structured plan for regularly moving money from your business to personal wealth vehicles. Most entrepreneurs handle profit distributions reactively, taking money out when the business has extra cash or personal expenses demand it. This reactive approach leads to inconsistent wealth-building at best and wealth stagnation at worst.

Your profit distribution strategy transforms this haphazard approach into a systematic process that happens automatically, regardless of what's happening in your business from day to day. It creates a non-negotiable commitment to building personal wealth alongside your business growth rather than postponing wealth-building until some future date that never arrives.

The first step in designing your strategy is determining your **optimal distribution percentage**—the portion of business profit you should transfer to personal wealth vehicles. This percentage varies based on your business type, growth goals, cash flow patterns, and personal financial situation. As a starting point, most established businesses should aim to distribute 30% to 50% of net profit to the owner for wealth-building, while earlier-stage companies might target 15% to 25%.

To calculate your percentage, start with your business's average monthly profit over the past year. Then subtract three numbers:

1. The amount needed for critical reinvestment to maintain growth
2. The amount needed for tax reserves
3. The amount needed for cash flow fluctuations

The remainder represents profit you could distribute without harming the business. Divide this by your total profit to find your optimal distribution percentage.

For example, if your business averages $30,000 monthly profit and needs $10,000 for growth investments, $6,000 for tax reserves, and $4,000 for cash flow coverage, you have $10,000 available for distribution. This gives you an optimal distribution percentage of 33% ($10,000 ÷ $30,000). This amount becomes your target for systematic wealth transfers.

The second step is creating your **distribution timing framework.** This determines how frequently you'll move money from business to personal accounts. The most effective approach for most entrepreneurs is either a monthly or quarterly distribution schedule. This rhythm creates consistent wealth-building momentum and prevents the business from absorbing funds that should be building your personal fortune.

Your distribution timing framework should align with your business's cash flow. If your business has predictable monthly and quarterly revenue, this works well. If you have more seasonal patterns, you might use a percentage-based approach where you transfer a set percentage of each month's profit rather than a fixed dollar amount. This adapts your distributions to business realities while maintaining the discipline of regular transfers.

One client with a seasonal landscaping business implemented a modified approach. During their eight busy months, they distributed 40% of profits monthly to the owner's wealth accounts. During their four slower months, they reduced this to 15% to preserve business cash flow. This flexible but systematic approach allowed consistent wealth-building while respecting business cash needs. Just to be clear, your distribution timing should be best suited for you. There is no hard and fast rule here.

The third step is establishing your **distribution pathway**—the route money takes from business accounts to personal wealth vehicles. This pathway should minimize taxes while maximizing long-term growth potential. For many entrepreneurs, the process involves taking multiple steps rather than simply transferring money to a personal checking account, where it might be spent rather than invested.

An effective distribution pathway might look like this: Business profit flows first to a dedicated profit hold account in the business. From there, a predetermined percentage moves to the owner as a combination of salary, distributions, or retirement plan contributions based on tax efficiency. These funds then automatically transfer to designated investment accounts rather than personal spending accounts. This creates a direct pipeline from business profit to wealth-building assets with minimal opportunity for leakage.

The fourth step is implementing **distribution automation**—setting up systems that execute your strategy without requiring constant decisions or willpower. This typically involves automatic transfers between accounts on predetermined dates, investment auto-deposits, and clear rules for handling extra profit beyond your baseline distributions.

One business owner set up a system where 35% of each month's profit automatically transferred to a separate business account on the twenty-fifth. On the first of the following month, the funds were transferred to his personal accounts as a combination of salary and distribution, according to a formula that his accountant and chief wealth officer determined. On the third of each month, his personal accounts automatically invested 80% in predetermined assets. This automation ensured that wealth-building happened consistently without requiring monthly decisions.

The final step is creating **distribution protection rules**—guidelines that determine when you might temporarily modify your distribution strategy during business challenges. You should establish these rules during good times, not create them reactively during a crisis. They specify exactly what business circumstances would trigger a reduction in distributions and how quickly you'll return to your standard strategy when conditions improve.

Effective Distribution Protection Rules might state that distributions will reduce to 15% of profit if business cash reserves drop below two months of operating expenses and return to the standard percentage when reserves rebuild to three months of expenses. Predetermining these rules prevents emotional decisions that might unnecessarily halt your wealth-building during temporary business fluctuations.

Your complete profit distribution strategy combines these elements into a cohesive system that consistently moves money from business success to personal wealth. It respects business cash flow needs while making wealth-building a non-negotiable priority rather than an afterthought. When fully implemented, it creates the critical bridge between making money in your business and building lasting personal wealth.

The Entrepreneur's Compensation Framework

How you pay yourself forms a crucial part of your Wealth Transfer Protocol. Most entrepreneurs set their pay based on their living expenses or what they think they can take from the business. This reactive approach ignores the powerful tax, wealth-building, and business structural advantages of a strategic compensation framework.

The Entrepreneur's Compensation Framework optimizes how you extract value from your business across three key components: salary, distributions, and work-optional (retirement) contributions. By carefully balancing these components based on your situation, you can dramatically increase the wealth-building power of every dollar your business generates.

The first component is strategic salary setting. Your salary isn't just about covering living expenses—it's a powerful tax and wealth-building tool. Setting it too low or too high can cost you tens of thousands in unnecessary taxes and missed wealth-building opportunities. The optimal approach varies based on your business entity type and personal financial situation.

For S corporation owners, the IRS requires you to take a "reasonable salary" before taking tax-advantaged distributions. Many entrepreneurs set this salary either too low (risking IRS scrutiny) or too high (paying unnecessary payroll taxes). The optimal strategy is typically setting your salary at the lower end of what's defensible as reasonable for your role and industry, allowing more profit to flow through as distributions that avoid the 15.3% self-employment tax.

One business owner was paying herself a $175,000 salary from her S corporation. After analyzing industry compensation data, we determined that $120,000 was still clearly reasonable for her role. Reducing her salary to this level while taking the difference as distributions saved her over $8,400 annually in payroll taxes—money that went directly into her investment accounts to build wealth.

For C corporation owners, the strategy often reverses. Taking more as salary (which is deductible to the corporation), and less as dividends (which create double taxation) can be more tax-efficient. The optimal balance depends on corporate and personal tax brackets, other income sources, and retirement plan opportunities. This analysis should be conducted annually as tax laws and your situation change.

The second component is distribution structuring. Beyond your salary, how you take profit distributions significantly impacts your wealth-building capacity. The key is creating a structured distribution plan rather than taking money randomly when the business has extra cash or personal expenses arise.

Effective distribution structuring includes setting a percentage of profit that automatically transfers to your personal accounts each month or quarter. This creates wealth-building consistency and prevents business expenses from expanding to consume all available cash. It also includes establishing a clear division between distributions for living expenses and distributions specifically for wealth-building, typically by directing them to separate personal accounts.

One entrepreneur implemented a three-tier distribution structure:

- Tier 1 covered basic living expenses through a consistent monthly transfer.
- Tier 2 provided quarterly distributions based on business performance, directed to investment accounts.
- Tier 3 created annual windfall distributions from excess profit that funded larger investment opportunities or major wealth steps.

This structured approach enabled business success by systematically building personal wealth rather than just enabling lifestyle expansion.

The third component is work-optional (retirement) maximization. Tax-advantaged retirement vehicles offer entrepreneurs powerful wealth-building tools that most don't fully utilize. The right retirement strategy can allow you to transfer significantly more money from business to personal wealth at lower tax rates than other compensation methods.

For many established entrepreneurs, advanced options like cash balance plans can allow annual retirement contributions of $200,000 or more—far beyond the limits of basic 401(k) plans. A solo 401(k) could also allow for contributions of $66,000 per year. These contributions reduce current business taxes while building substantial personal wealth in tax-advantaged accounts. The optimal retirement strategy depends on your business entity type, profit level, age, and other factors.

The fourth component is compensation timing. When you pay yourself matters almost as much as how much you pay yourself. Strategic timing of salary, distributions, and work-optional (retirement) contributions can significantly reduce tax burden and increase wealth-building efficiency.

Effective timing strategies include balancing distributions across tax years to manage brackets, accelerating or delaying income based on anticipated tax law changes, clustering deductions to maximize their impact, and aligning major distributions with investment opportunities. These approaches require planning but can add substantial wealth over time.

One client saved over $23,000 in taxes by delaying a large year-end distribution by just two weeks, pushing it into January of the following tax year, when she anticipated being in a lower bracket due to business investments. This tax saving went directly into her wealth-building accounts, effectively increasing the wealth-building power of that distribution by nearly 30%.

The final component is compensation evolution—adjusting your framework as your business and wealth grow. The optimal strategy for a startup differs dramatically from that of a mature business. As your business evolves, your compensation structure should shift to maximize wealth-building efficiency at each stage.

In early business stages, you might focus on establishing a baseline salary that creates personal financial stability while reinvesting heavily in growth. As the business matures, you would shift toward maximizing tax-advantaged distributions and retirement contributions. In later stages, you might structure compensation to support business exit planning or legacy goals.

Your complete Entrepreneur's Compensation Framework integrates these components into a cohesive strategy that evolves with your business. When properly implemented, it dramatically increases the after-tax wealth you can build from the same business profit. It transforms compensation from a simple paycheck into a powerful wealth-building system that systematically transfers value from your business to personal assets you control.

Implementing the Five-Minute Monthly Wealth Habit

The most powerful wealth transfer protocol in the world won't help you if you don't consistently implement it. This is where most entrepreneurs fail. They create good plans but get too busy running their businesses to execute them systematically. The Five-Minute Monthly Wealth Habit solves this problem by turning wealth transfer from an occasional event into a monthly practice that requires minimal time but produces extraordinary results.

This simple habit has transformed struggling business owners into multimillionaires not by creating complex new strategies but by consistently executing fundamental wealth-building actions regardless of business chaos. It works because it focuses on the critical few actions that drive most wealth-building results while requiring so little time that even the busiest entrepreneur can maintain it.

The core of this habit is the monthly wealth transfer review—a five-minute process you complete each month. This review consists of five simple steps that keep your wealth transfer system on track regardless of what's happening in your business or personal life.

Step 1 - Track profits: Each month, take sixty seconds to record the month's business revenue, major expenses, and approximate profit. This will come straight from your monthly CWO dashboard's critical four. It's a quick reality check that keeps profit awareness at the forefront of your mind. When you track profit monthly, you make better decisions that protect your wealth-building capacity.

One business owner began tracking profit on a simple spreadsheet each month. Within months, this habit helped him identify a client project that was consistently unprofitable despite high revenue. Adjusting the pricing on this project added $4,300 monthly to his bottom line—money that flowed directly into his wealth transfer system.

Step 2 - Verify transfers: Take sixty seconds to confirm that your most recent scheduled wealth transfer happened. Check that money moved from business to personal accounts according to your distribution strategy. If it didn't, identify the reason and take immediate corrective action instead of ignoring it.

This verification step catches problems quickly before they derail your wealth-building. One entrepreneur discovered that his automatic transfers had stopped because his business account information had changed after a bank merger. Because he caught this within days rather than months, he avoided a significant gap in his wealth-building momentum.

Step 3—Allocate wealth: Take sixty seconds to make sure that money transferred to personal accounts moves promptly to appropriate investment vehicles rather than sitting in cash or being absorbed by lifestyle expenses. This might mean confirming an automatic investment contribution or manually moving money to specific accounts.

This step prevents one of the most common wealth-building leaks—money that transfers from business to personal accounts but never makes it into investments.

One client realized through this daily check that over $30,000 had accumulated in her personal checking account rather than being invested according to her plan. Correcting this oversight and implementing automatic investment transfers added significantly to her long-term wealth trajectory.

Step 4 – Identify obstacles: Take sixty seconds to identify any upcoming business situations that might threaten your wealth transfers, then develop a quick plan to address them. This proactive approach prevents business challenges from automatically derailing your wealth-building.

One business owner identified an upcoming cash-flow gap due to delayed client payments. Rather than automatically suspending his wealth transfers as he would have done previously, he arranged a short-term line of credit to cover business needs during this temporary gap. This allowed his wealth-building transfers to continue uninterrupted despite the business challenge.

Step 5 – Recognize opportunities: Take sixty seconds to identify any unusual business profit opportunities that could fund additional wealth transfers beyond your standard plan. This lets you capture wealth-building potential from business windfalls rather than allowing them to dissipate through increased business spending.

One entrepreneur noticed an unusually profitable month when a large project was completed. Rather than letting this extra profit sit in the business account, where it would likely be absorbed by expanded expenses, she immediately transferred 40% to her investment accounts, significantly accelerating her wealth-building that quarter.

The power of this five-minute habit comes from its consistency and focus on the critical few actions that drive wealth-building results. By spending just five minutes on these steps, you create a wealth-transfer system that runs automatically regardless of business chaos. The habit serves as a bridge between understanding what needs to be done and consistently executing it.

To successfully implement this habit, connect it to a monthly routine that you consistently engage in. We do this with our clients on our monthly sixty-minute CWO call. By anchoring your wealth habit to an established routine, you dramatically increase the likelihood of maintaining it long-term.

You can also create simple accountability by tracking your habit completion. A basic calendar where you mark that you've completed the five-minute review creates visual momentum that helps you stay consistent. After several months, the habit becomes almost automatic—something you feel uncomfortable skipping because it's now part of your identity as a wealth-building entrepreneur.

The entrepreneurs who implement this habit see dramatically different results from those who approach wealth transfer sporadically. One client who maintained this habit for three years built over $1.2 million in investments outside his business despite modest annual profits. Another individual increased her personal net worth by over 400% in five years while operating the same business at approximately the same profit level. The difference wasn't new strategies. These two clients consistently executed fundamental wealth transfers regardless of business circumstances.

Chapter 3 Recap: Creating Your Wealth Transfer System

You now understand the critical importance of having a systematic process for moving money from your business to personal wealth-building assets. The Wealth Transfer Protocol, which we talked about in this chapter, serves as the crucial link that converts business success into personal wealth—a connection that most entrepreneurs fail to establish.

Key Insights

The Wealth Transfer Gap

- Business profit ≠ personal wealth unless systematically transferred.
- Without a deliberate system, even profitable businesses fail to create lasting wealth for their owners.
- Reliance on business profit alone keeps entrepreneurs financially vulnerable.

The Wealth Transfer Protocol

- A structured system that moves profit from your business to personal wealth-building assets.
- Ensures financial independence by converting business success into personal net worth.

Profit Distribution Strategy

- Design a plan to move profit effectively:
  - **Optimal Distribution Percentage**: Calculate based on your business's situation.
  - **Timing Framework**: Establish regular intervals for transferring profit.
  - **Tax-Efficient Pathway**: Minimize tax drag during transfers.
  - **Automation**: Set up systems for seamless, consistent transfers.
  - **Protection Rules**: Safeguard distributions during business challenges.

Entrepreneur's Compensation Framework

- Optimize how you pay yourself through:
  - Strategic salary setting (based on business entity type).
  - Consistent, structured profit distributions.
  - Retirement maximization using tax-advantaged contributions.
  - Timing strategies to minimize tax burden.
  - Evolving the framework as your business grows.

Five-Minute Quarterly Wealth Habit

- A simple practice to maintain consistency in wealth-building:
  - Assess your wealth transfer system quarterly.
  - Transform wealth-building into a disciplined, habitual process.

Action Steps

1. Document Your Current Wealth Transfer Process

- Map out how money currently moves from your business to personal accounts.
- Identify gaps or inconsistencies in your approach.

2. Identify Wealth Leaks

- Look for areas where profit is trapped or diverted, such as:
  - Excess business cash reserves.
  - Unnecessary expenses.

  - Tax inefficiencies.
  - Personal spending that depletes distributions before investment.

3. Design Your Profit Distribution Strategy

- Calculate your optimal distribution percentage.
- Establish a timing framework for regular transfers.
- Map out a tax-efficient pathway for moving funds.
- Automate the process for consistency.
- Create protection rules to safeguard distributions during tough times.

4. Optimize Your Compensation Framework

- Work with your tax professional to balance salary, distributions, and retirement contributions.
- Implement systems to automate compensation decisions.

5. Implement the Five-Minute Quarterly Wealth Habit

- Integrate this habit into an existing routine (e.g., monthly financial check-ins).
- Track progress to ensure your wealth transfer system operates smoothly and consistently.

Key Takeaways for Transformation

- **Bridge the Gap**: The Wealth Transfer Protocol connects business success to personal financial independence.
- **Start Now**: Wealth transfer isn't a future goal—it begins today with the profit you already generate.
- **Consistency Wins**: Regular, deliberate transfers build lasting wealth, no matter the size of your business.

Next Steps in the Book

- Learn advanced strategies for tax-efficient wealth extraction.
- Explore methods to protect and grow your personal wealth outside the business.
- Build a financial system that ensures long-term security and independence.

Chapter 4
The Tax Reduction Code

Why Entrepreneurs Overpay Taxes

Most entrepreneurs pay far more in taxes than they legally need to. This isn't because they want to give extra money to the government. It happens because of fundamental mistakes in how they structure their businesses, time their transactions, and document their activities. These mistakes cost business owners tens or even hundreds of thousands of dollars every single year.

The biggest mistake entrepreneurs make is treating tax planning as an event rather than a system. They meet with their CPA once a year in March or April, looking backward at money already earned and spent. By then, it's too late to implement most of the strategies that could have saved significant tax dollars. The tax return becomes a historical document that simply calculates how much you owe based on decisions already made rather than a strategic tool for building wealth.

I worked with a business owner who made over $800,000 in profit but didn't talk to his accountant until tax filing time. By then, he had no options left. He wrote a check for over $270,000 in taxes. We implemented a proper tax planning system. The next year, he made $950,000 in profit but paid only $180,000 in taxes. The difference didn't come from doing anything aggressive or risky. It was just from making decisions with tax consequences at the right time rather than after the fact.

The second major mistake is using the wrong business structure or outgrowing your current structure without updating it. Many entrepreneurs start with whatever entity their initial lawyer recommended, often a simple LLC or S corporation. As their business evolves and grows, this structure becomes increasingly inefficient for tax purposes, but they never revisit the decision.

Entity structure isn't just a legal consideration—it's the foundation of your tax strategy. It is the difference between optimal and suboptimal structure. This often results in entrepreneurs paying 10% to 15% more in unnecessary taxes on their income. That's $100,000 to $150,000 a year for just $1 million in profit—money that could be building your personal wealth instead of funding government programs.

The third critical mistake is failing to integrate business and personal tax planning. Most entrepreneurs have a business accountant and a separate personal financial advisor. Neither of them has a comprehensive understanding of the situation. The business accountant may recommend strategies that save business taxes but might increase personal taxes. The personal advisor suggests approaches that make sense for employees but not business owners. The result: tax strategies that work against each other instead of a unified plan.

One client came to me after taking a $200,000 distribution from his S corporation in December based on his business accountant's recommendation to get the money out of the business. But his personal tax situation meant this distribution pushed him into a higher tax bracket, costing an extra $18,000 in taxes. Had the two sides of his financial life been properly coordinated, he could have timed this distribution differently or used alternative strategies to achieve the same goals without the added tax cost.

The fourth mistake is poor documentation and recordkeeping. The tax code offers many deductions and strategies that are perfectly legal but require proper documentation. Without systematic recordkeeping, entrepreneurs leave thousands of dollars of deductions unclaimed each year simply because they can't properly substantiate them during an audit.

A restaurant owner I worked with was taking only about 60% of the legitimate deductions available to her business because she didn't have systems to track and document the rest. After implementing proper documentation protocols, she increased her deductions by over $80,000 annually without taking on a single aggressive position. These were all deductions she was legally entitled to but had been missing due to poor recordkeeping.

The fifth and perhaps most costly mistake is making business decisions without considering tax implications. Entrepreneurs often decide when to buy equipment, hire employees, expand locations, or sell assets based purely on business factors without understanding the tax consequences. This disconnected decision-making frequently leads to paying tens of thousands more in taxes than necessary.

These mistakes compound over time. An entrepreneur who consistently overpays taxes by $50,000 annually doesn't just lose that money—they lose all the future wealth they could have created through investment. Over twenty years, that $50,000 annual tax overpayment costs over $2.3 million in lost wealth potential when you consider reasonable investment returns. This is why tax strategy forms a critical component of the Wealth Transfer Protocol we discussed in the previous chapter.

Entity Optimization for Tax Efficiency

Your business entity structure forms the foundation of your tax strategy. It's like the foundation of a house—get it wrong, and everything built on top becomes unstable and inefficient. However, most entrepreneurs tend to overlook their entity structure after they form their business, resulting in significant financial losses as their business develops.

The first principle of entity optimization asserts that there is no universally applicable solution. The right structure depends on your business model, income level, growth plans, personal financial situation, and wealth-building goals. What works for one entrepreneur may not work for you, even if you're in the same industry.

For businesses with under $250,000 in profit, a single-entity structure often makes sense. This might be an LLC taxed as an S corporation, which allows you to save on self-employment taxes by taking a reasonable salary plus distributions. This simple structure works well for many service businesses, consultants, and professionals in early growth stages.

One consultant I worked with was operating as a sole proprietor, paying the full 15.3% self-employment tax on all her income. By switching to an S corporation structure and taking $90,000 as salary with the remaining $110,000 as distributions, she immediately saved over $16,000 in taxes. This simple entity change created a 16% instant raise without changing anything about her business operations.

As your business grows beyond $250,000 in profit, multi-entity structures often become more tax-efficient. This might involve separating different business functions into distinct entities, each with its own tax treatment. For example, you might have an operating company taxed as an S corporation, a management company taxed as a C corporation, and a holding company for assets taxed as a partnership.

A manufacturing business owner implemented this multi-entity approach, moving their equipment into a separate LLC that leased it back to the operating company. This structure created legitimate deductions for the operating business while moving profits to an entity with more favorable tax treatment. The net result was annual tax savings of over $93,000 without changing the underlying business operations.

For businesses with over $1 million in profit, even more sophisticated structures become viable. These might include domestic holding companies, defined benefit plans, captive insurance arrangements, or specialized trusts. While more complex to establish and maintain, these structures can create tax savings that reach into the hundreds of thousands annually for highly profitable businesses.

One technology company owner with $2.8 million in annual profit implemented a comprehensive multi-entity structure, including a management C corporation, an operating S corporation, and a specialized retirement plan. This integrated approach reduced their tax bill by over

$430,000 annually compared to their previous single-entity structure. Over five years, this created over $2.1 million in additional wealth for the owner.

The second principle of entity optimization is that your structure should evolve as your business grows. The entity that perfectly served your needs at $300,000 in revenue becomes increasingly inefficient as you reach $3 million or $30 million. Smart entrepreneurs review their entity structure annually and make adjustments as their business changes.

This evolution doesn't always mean greater complexity. Occasionally, it means simplifying or consolidating entities that no longer serve a purpose. The key is that your entity structure should be intentionally designed to support your current business reality rather than remaining static as a relic of your early decisions.

The third principle is that entity optimization goes beyond just tax considerations. Your structure should also support asset protection, liability management, and wealth transfer goals. The ideal structure creates tax efficiency while also protecting your assets from potential business risks and facilitating eventual wealth transfer to family or a business exit.

A service business owner created a structure that not only saved over $70,000 annually in taxes but also protected their personal assets from business liabilities and created a clear pathway for eventually transferring the business to their children. This integrated approach addressed multiple financial goals through a single, coherent entity strategy.

The fourth principle is that implementation timing matters enormously. Entity changes have tax implications based on when they occur during the calendar or fiscal year. Making these changes at the wrong time can significantly reduce their benefit or even create additional tax burdens in the transition year.

One business owner decided to convert from an S corporation to a C corporation structure based on the new lower corporate tax rates. But they made this change in November without properly planning for the transition. This timing mistake created an unexpected $47,000 tax bill that could have been avoided if they had waited just two months and implemented the change at the beginning of their next fiscal year.

The final principle is that entity optimization requires specialized expertise. This isn't an area for general business attorneys or standard accountants. The tax code contains over 75,000 pages, and the sections relating to business entities are among the most complex. Working with professionals who specialize in tax-efficient entity structuring for businesses in your revenue range is essential for optimal results.

Entity optimization isn't about finding loopholes or aggressive tax positions. It's about structuring your business in full compliance with tax law to minimize your legal tax burden. The government creates tax incentives for business activities through the entity structures it recognizes. Smart entrepreneurs simply organize their legitimate business activities in ways that maximize these intended benefits.

Strategic Tax Planning vs. Tax Preparation

The distinction between tax preparation and strategic tax planning is significant. Tax preparation looks backward at what has already happened. Strategic tax planning looks forward and actively shapes financial decisions to minimize tax burden. This distinction might seem subtle, but it represents tens or even hundreds of thousands of dollars in wealth-building potential for successful entrepreneurs.

Tax preparation is what most CPAs and entrepreneurs do. They run their business throughout the year, making decisions based on operational needs. Then they gather their financial records in March or April and hand them to an accountant, who prepares returns that calculate how much they owe based on what has already happened. The accountant might find some deductions the entrepreneur overlooked, but fundamentally, this backward-looking process can only document history, not change it.

Strategic tax planning takes an entirely different approach. It starts with understanding your business and personal financial goals for the coming years. Then it creates a proactive plan for structuring transactions, timing income and expenses, and documenting activities to legally minimize taxes while supporting those goals. This forward-looking process shapes financial decisions throughout the year rather than just recording their consequences after the fact.

The difference in results is dramatic. Entrepreneurs who engage in strategic tax planning typically pay 15% to 30% less in taxes than those who focus only on preparation. For $500,000 of business profit, this difference often represents $75,000 to $150,000 annually in tax savings—money that builds your wealth rather than going into the government's pocket.

I worked with two business owners in the same industry with nearly identical revenue and profit. One focused only on tax preparation, meeting with his accountant once a year to file returns. The other implemented strategic tax planning with quarterly strategy sessions and monthly implementation checks. After three years, the second owner had paid $347,000 less in total taxes despite earning slightly more. This difference created over $420,000 in additional wealth through the investment of those tax savings.

Strategic tax planning has five core components that distinguish it from simple preparation. The first is timing optimization—strategically controlling when you recognize income and expenses to minimize the tax burden across multiple years rather than just the current one. This might mean accelerating deductions into high-income years, deferring income into lower-income years, or spreading large transactions across tax years to avoid bracket jumps.

The second component is income characterization—structuring your business activities so that your income receives the most favorable tax treatment possible. Different types of income face dramatically different tax rates. Ordinary income can be taxed at up to 37% federally, while qualified dividends and long-term capital gains max out at 20%. Self-employment income faces an additional 15.3% tax that other income types avoid.

A real estate entrepreneur was earning all his income as ordinary business profit through an LLC, facing combined federal and self-employment taxes exceeding 40%. Through strategic planning, he restructured his activities so that a portion qualified as long-term capital gains and another portion as passive rental income not subject to self-employment tax. This characterization change reduced his tax rate on much of his income by almost half without changing his underlying business activities.

The third component is deduction maximization—systematically identifying, documenting, and optimizing all available business deductions. This goes far beyond the obvious expenses most entrepreneurs already claim.

It involves structuring business activities to qualify for enhanced deductions, implementing documentation systems that substantiate borderline expenses, and timing discretionary expenses for maximum tax impact.

A restaurant owner implemented a strategic deduction system that properly documented meals, travel, vehicle use, home office, and technology expenses according to IRS requirements. This systematic approach increased her legitimate deductions by over $35,000 annually compared to her previous informal tracking. The tax savings directly increased her wealth-building capacity without changing her spending.

The fourth component is work-optional (retirement) strategy integration—using tax-advantaged retirement vehicles as part of your overall tax plan rather than as a separate consideration. For entrepreneurs, specialized options, like defined benefit plans, cash balance plans, or solo 401(k)s, can allow annual tax-deferred contributions far exceeding standard limits, sometimes reaching $200,000 or more, depending on age and income.

One owner of a professional services firm implemented a cash balance plan that allowed him to contribute $175,000 annually to his retirement while creating an immediate tax deduction for his business. This reduced his annual tax bill by over $65,000 while rapidly building his retirement wealth in a tax-advantaged account. Over ten years, this strategy is projected to create over $1 million in additional retirement assets compared to his previous approach.

The fifth component is multi-entity coordination—making all entities in your business structure work together for optimal tax efficiency. This means coordinating the timing of transactions between entities, properly documenting intercompany agreements, and ensuring that each entity serves its intended tax purpose while maintaining proper separation.

A business owner with three separate entities was making decisions for each one independently. By implementing coordinated planning across all entities, he was able to time distributions, allocate expenses, and structure agreements between entities to reduce his overall tax burden by over $43,000 annually without changing the fundamental business operations.

Strategic tax planning isn't a one-time event. It is an ongoing process that adapts to changes in your business, personal financial situation, and tax laws. The most effective approach involves quarterly strategy sessions with your tax professional to review results, adjust plans, and identify new opportunities. With these regular check-ins, your tax strategy aligns with business reality rather than becoming an abstract plan that is never fully implemented.

The entrepreneurs who benefit most from strategic tax planning are those who integrate it into their regular business decision-making rather than treating it as a separate financial function. They consider tax implications before making major business moves, consult their tax strategist about timing and structuring transactions, and maintain the documentation systems needed to support their tax positions.

This integrated approach transforms taxes from an inevitable burden into a manageable expense that responds to strategic planning just like any other business cost. The result is significantly more wealth retained and invested rather than surrendered unnecessarily to tax authorities.

The Entrepreneur's Tax Calendar: A Quarter-by-Quarter Guide

Most entrepreneurs think about taxes only when filing deadlines approach. This reactive approach guarantees missed opportunities for strategic tax savings. The **Entrepreneur's Tax Calendar** creates a proactive, quarterly system for implementing tax strategies before critical deadlines. This method ensures that you take the right actions at the right times to optimize your tax savings throughout the year.

This isn't about compliance dates. (Your accountant tracks those.) Instead, it's about strategic decision points that can significantly reduce your tax burden. By addressing these priorities each quarter, you'll transform your tax planning into a proactive, wealth-building system.

Q1: Laying the Foundation (January–March)

January: Strategy Finalization Month

- Document your annual tax strategy based on projections for the coming year.
- Review last year's results, update income and expense forecasts, and finalize strategies and savings targets.
- Create a written tax plan with actionable steps assigned to each quarter.

Example: One business owner developed a detailed tax strategy in January with their accountant, identifying over $120,000 in potential savings. This road map resulted in accountability and proactive implementation throughout the year.

February: Entity Evaluation Month

- Review your business structure for tax efficiency.
- Implement any necessary entity changes (e.g., S corporation election) to maximize benefits for the current tax year.
- Make these changes within the first seventy-five days of the year to apply them retroactively.

Example: A service business owner restructured in February based on January's planning session. By applying the changes early, they saved over $30,000 compared to waiting later in the year.

March: Work-Optional (Retirement) Strategy Month

- Establish or adjust tax-advantaged retirement plans (e.g., SEP IRA, 401(k), or defined benefit plans).
- Early implementation maximizes tax-deferred growth and ensures compliance with plan setup deadlines.

Example: An entrepreneur set up a defined benefit plan in March, enabling her to contribute $150,000 annually while receiving significant tax deductions. Starting early gave her nine extra months of tax-deferred growth.

Q2: Midyear Course Corrections (April–June)

April: Quarterly Review Month

- Compare Q1 results with your projections.
- Adjust your tax strategy to address higher-than-expected profit or other deviations.
- Consider accelerating deductions or increasing retirement contributions to offset income spikes.

Example: A business owner noticed that Q1 profits were 30% above projections. By accelerating equipment purchases and retirement contributions, they saved $27,000 in taxes.

May: Income Timing Month

- Strategize the timing of income recognition for cash-basis businesses.
- If next year's income will be lower, delay client billings to January. If this year offers more deductions, accelerate income into December.

Example: A consultant adjusted her billing schedule in May, pushing payments into the next tax year when she expected a lower tax bracket. This simple move saved $14,000 in taxes.

June: Midyear Estimation Month

- Conduct a detailed midyear tax projection.
- Identify potential tax issues and implement solutions with six months remaining in the year.
- Consider strategies like accelerating expenses, increasing contributions, or shifting income.

Example: A business owner's June projection revealed higher-than-expected income. Early action—including accelerating investments and income-shifting strategies—saved them $47,000 in taxes.

Q3: Strategic Adjustments (July–September)

July: Family Tax Integration Month

- Implement strategies involving family members, such as employing children or establishing family limited partnerships.
- Enforce proper documentation and IRS compliance for these strategies to succeed.

Example: A business owner employed his teenage children in legitimate roles, shifting $18,000 of income to each child's lower tax bracket and funding Roth IRAs. This strategy reduced taxes while building family wealth.

August: Deduction Acceleration Month

- Identify large deduction opportunities requiring lead time, such as cost segregation studies, R&D credits, or energy-efficiency improvements.
- Start these processes now to ensure completion before year-end.

Example: A property owner initiated a cost segregation study in August, accelerating $120,000 in depreciation deductions. Starting early meant the savings were realized that year.

September: Third-Quarter Adjustment Month

- Review year-to-date results and make final strategic adjustments before Q4.
- Accelerate planned expenses or defer income, if beneficial, to optimize your tax position.

Example: A business owner noticed a 25% income increase during their September review. By accelerating $200,000 of equipment purchases, they saved $74,000 in taxes through bonus depreciation.

Q4: Year-End Optimization (October–December)

October: State Tax Strategy Month

- Implement strategies to minimize state taxes, such as restructuring operations or establishing nexus in lower-tax jurisdictions.
- Focus on state-specific strategies that can save 5% to 13% of business income.

Example: A multistate business owner restructured their operations in October, reducing state tax liability by $35,000 annually without altering business activities.

November: Finalizing Year-End Strategies

- Complete a final tax projection and prioritize high-impact strategies.
- Focus on actions like charitable contributions, retirement plan maximization, or equipment purchases that can be completed quickly.

Example: A business owner identified $83,000 in potential deductions during their November planning session and implemented $67,000 of them, reducing their tax bill by $24,000.

December: Implementation Completion Month

- Execute all remaining year-end strategies for proper documentation and compliance.
- Coordinate with vendors, clients, and financial institutions to finalize transactions.

Example: An entrepreneur completed six strategies in December, including prepaying expenses, deferring income, and maximizing retirement contributions. These moves reduced their tax bill by $63,000.

Conclusion: Build a Proactive Tax System

The **Entrepreneur's Tax Calendar** turns tax planning into a proactive, quarterly system. By addressing key decision points each quarter, you stay ahead of deadlines and maximize your tax savings. With this approach, your tax planning isn't just about compliance. It's a powerful tool for reducing your tax burden and building wealth.

Chapter 4 Recap: Implementing Your Tax Reduction Strategy

You've now discovered the fundamental principles of the Tax Reduction Code—a systematic approach that allows entrepreneurs to minimize their tax burden while building personal wealth. Let's recap what you've learned and outline your immediate action steps to implement these strategies in your own business and personal finances.

Key Insights

The Tax Planning Problem

- Most entrepreneurs overpay taxes because they:
  - Treat tax planning as a one-time event, not a system.
  - Use outdated or inefficient business structures.
  - Fail to integrate business and personal tax strategies.
  - Maintain poor documentation for deductions.
  - Make decisions without considering tax implications.

Entity Optimization for Tax Efficiency

- Your business structure forms the foundation of your tax strategy.
- The right entity depends on your income, goals, and business model.
- Structures should evolve with your business growth and financial goals.
- Implementation requires specialized expertise and careful timing.

Strategic Tax Planning vs. Tax Preparation

- **Tax Preparation**: Focuses on compliance and filing.
- **Strategic Tax Planning**: Proactively reduces your tax burden by 15%-30% through:
  - **Timing Optimization**: Align actions with tax deadlines.

- **Income Characterization**: Classify income for lower tax rates.
- **Deduction Maximization**: Identify and document all eligible deductions.
- **Retirement Strategy Integration**: Use tax-advantaged accounts effectively.
- **Multi-Entity Coordination**: Optimize across multiple business entities.

Entrepreneur's Tax Calendar

- A proactive, quarter-by-quarter system for implementing tax strategies.
- Ensures you capture tax opportunities at the right time.
- Prevents missed savings from delayed or reactive decisions.

Action Steps

1. Schedule a Business Entity Review

- Work with a tax strategist to evaluate your current business structure.
- Ensure it aligns with your income level, business model, and wealth-building goals.
- Update outdated structures to unlock potential tax savings.

2. Create Your Tax Strategy Document

- Develop a comprehensive plan for the year, including:
    - Strategies to implement.
    - Implementation timelines.
    - Responsible parties.
    - Expected tax savings from each strategy.
- Use this document as a roadmap for all tax-related decisions.

3. Build Your Tax Calendar

- Set dates for implementing strategies from your tax plan.
- Add reminders at least two weeks before each action.
- Use the calendar to track progress and stay proactive.

4. Identify Your Top 3 Tax-Saving Opportunities

- Focus on high-impact strategies, such as:
    - Retirement plan optimization.
    - Business entity restructuring.
    - Improved documentation for deductions.
- Prioritize these opportunities to maximize immediate results.

5. Work with the Right Advisors

- Partner with a tax strategist who understands integrated business and personal tax planning.
- Ensure they collaborate with your other financial advisors to align strategies with your overall wealth-building goals.

Key Takeaways for Transformation

- **Reduce Tax Burden**: Strategic planning keeps more profits flowing to your personal wealth.
- **Start Now:** Proactive, consistent implementation yields the greatest results.
- **Evolve Over Time**: Regular reviews ensure your strategy adapts to changes in your business, tax laws, and personal goals.

Next Steps in the Book

- Discover advanced strategies for wealth protection and risk management.
- Learn how to build tax-efficient investment vehicles that grow outside your business.
- Explore methods for scaling your wealth transfer and tax reduction systems as your business grows.

Chapter 5

The Personal Wealth Engine

Beyond the Business: Your Personal Balance Sheet

Your business makes good money. You work hard for it. But there's a big difference between having a business that makes money and being wealthy. Your business income can make you *rich;* however, it may not make you *wealthy.* True wealth exists outside your business on your personal balance sheet. This is where most entrepreneurs go wrong. They pour everything into growing their business while their personal balance sheet stays thin and weak.

Think about it this way: Your business balance sheet shows what your company owns and owes. Your personal balance sheet (net worth statement) shows what you own and owe, which is separate from your business. Many successful entrepreneurs have impressive business balance sheets but surprisingly weak personal ones. They might run companies worth millions while having little saved or invested in their name. This can lead to a risky scenario where all their financial resources are concentrated in a single entity. Have you ever heard the expression "Don't put all your eggs in one basket"?

I recently collaborated with Michael, who over the course of eight years built a technology company valued at $5 million. His business looked great on paper. But when we examined his personal balance sheet, we found less than $200,000 in assets outside the business. Even though he'd drawn a healthy salary for years, almost everything went to an expensive lifestyle or back into the company. His entire financial future depended on the continued success of his business in a rapidly changing industry.

Building a strong personal balance sheet means systematically moving wealth from your business to assets you personally control. These assets then grow independently of your business, creating true financial security that doesn't depend on your company's performance. This wealth transfer doesn't happen by accident. It requires a deliberate system that works even when business demands your full attention.

The first step in building your personal balance sheet is knowing exactly where you stand today. Most entrepreneurs have only a vague idea of their personal net worth outside their business. They might know they have some money in retirement accounts or equity in their home, but few maintain a current, accurate picture of their complete financial position.

Create a simple personal balance sheet by listing everything you own in one column and everything you owe in another. Include all assets: cash, investments, retirement accounts, real estate equity, vehicles, and other valuables. Then list all liabilities: mortgages, loans, credit card balances, and other debts. Subtract what you owe from what you own to calculate your personal net worth, excluding your business value. We track our clients' personal net worth on the same CWO dashboard that monitors the critical four in their businesses.

This number often surprises entrepreneurs. Many discover that their personal net worth is much lower than expected, given their income level. One business owner, who earned over $500,000 annually for five years, was shocked to discover that his personal net worth outside the business was only $180,000. Despite earning millions over those years, he had little to show for it on his personal balance sheet.

The second step is establishing your Wealth Ratio—the relationship between your business value and personal assets. Calculate this by dividing your personal net worth (excluding your business) by your business value. For example, if your business is worth $2 million and your personal net worth is $400,000, your Wealth Ratio is 0.2 or 20%.

A healthy Wealth Ratio for established entrepreneurs typically falls between 0.5 and 2.0, meaning your personal wealth should be at least half your business value and ideally equal to or greater than your business value. This balance ensures that your financial future doesn't depend entirely on your company's continued success or eventual sale.

Most entrepreneurs I meet have Wealth Ratios below 0.3, indicating dangerous concentration in their business assets. One construction company owner I coached had built a business worth approximately $3.5 million but had personal assets worth only $420,000—a Wealth Ratio of just 0.12. His entire financial life depended on his company's performance in a volatile industry where new competitors constantly emerged.

The third step is creating your Personal Balance Sheet Growth Plan—a systematic approach to increasing your personal assets over time. This plan should include targets for growing your personal net worth independent of business growth. While your business might aim to increase revenue or profit by certain percentages, your personal plan focuses on building assets you control outside the company.

An effective Personal Balance Sheet Growth Plan includes monthly wealth transfer targets from business to personal accounts, asset allocation strategies for these transfers, and milestones for your Wealth Ratio improvement. For example, you might target transferring 30% of business profit to personal wealth vehicles monthly, with the goal of improving your Wealth Ratio from 0.2 to 0.5 within three years.

One business owner implemented a Personal Balance Sheet Growth Plan that systematically transferred $12,000 monthly from business profits to personal investment accounts. Over four years, this consistent approach increased her personal net worth from $350,000 to over $1.2 million while her business grew from $2.5 million to $4 million in value. Her Wealth Ratio improved from 0.14 to 0.3, still below ideal but moving in the right direction.

The fourth step is establishing your Wealth Freedom Number—the personal net worth you need to achieve financial independence, regardless of your business. This number represents the assets required to generate enough passive income to cover your lifestyle without depending on business income.

Calculate your Wealth Freedom Number by determining your annual lifestyle costs and multiplying by 25 (assuming a 4% safe withdrawal rate). For example, if you need $150,000 annually to maintain your lifestyle, your Wealth Freedom Number would be $3.75 million in personal assets. This becomes the ultimate target for your personal balance sheet growth.

Many entrepreneurs set business growth targets without ever calculating their personal Wealth Freedom Number. They work tirelessly to grow companies without knowing how much personal wealth they need to achieve financial independence. One business owner had been striving to build a $10 million company but discovered that his Wealth Freedom Number was only $2.2 million based on his desired lifestyle. This realization entirely changed his approach, shifting focus from maximum business growth to optimal wealth transfer.

The fifth step is implementing Balance Sheet Protection strategies that safeguard your growing personal assets from business risks, lawsuits, and other threats. As your personal balance sheet grows, protecting these assets becomes increasingly important.

Effective protection strategies include maintaining proper business entity structures that separate personal and business assets and having appropriate insurance coverage, including umbrella policies, and, in some cases, more advanced asset protection vehicles, like certain trusts or limited partnerships. The specific approach depends on your asset types, value, and risk exposure.

One entrepreneur had built significant personal wealth but kept it in accounts directly linked to his business banking relationship. When his company faced a cash flow crisis, his bank froze his personal accounts as well due to cross-collateralization agreements he hadn't carefully reviewed. Proper balance sheet protection would have prevented this situation by maintaining a clear separation between business and personal finances.

Building your personal balance sheet isn't about taking money your business needs for growth. It's about ensuring that a portion of the wealth your business creates is systematically transferred to assets you personally control. This creates true financial security that doesn't depend on your company's continued success or eventual sale. Your business becomes a wealth-creation engine rather than your only significant asset.

The Wealthy Entrepreneur's Investment Framework

Most investment advice wasn't created for entrepreneurs. It was designed for employees with steady paychecks and limited upside. Your situation is entirely different. You have a unique risk profile, irregular income patterns, and a significant investment already tied up in your business. You need an investment framework designed for wealth-building entrepreneurs.

The Wealthy Entrepreneur's Investment Framework addresses the special challenges and opportunities you face as a business owner. It recognizes that your investment strategy must complement your business rather than competing with it for returns. It accounts for the fact that you already have a significant investment in your company and need diversification rather than concentration. Most importantly, it works with your irregular income and unique risk profile rather than assuming steady contributions like most investment approaches.

The first principle of this framework is **risk balancing.** As an entrepreneur, you already take significant risks in your business. Your investment strategy should balance this risk rather than amplify it. This often means taking a different approach with your personal investments than traditional advisors might recommend for someone with a regular job.

The traditional advice assumes that your income comes from stable employment. As an entrepreneur, you're already taking enormous risk with your primary income source—your business. Your personal investments may need to provide stability to counterbalance this risk, not add to it by concentrating in high-risk assets.

The second principle is **liquidity layering.** Entrepreneurs need more accessible cash than employees because business opportunities and challenges can arise unexpectedly. Your investment strategy should create distinct liquidity layers with varying amounts of money accessible within different time frames.

An effective liquidity structure typically includes two layers: emergency capital available immediately (typically three to six months of personal expenses) and opportunity capital accessible within one to three months without significant penalties (typically six to twelve months of expenses).

One business owner maintained minimal cash reserves, keeping nearly everything invested for maximum growth. When a major client unexpectedly delayed payment, he faced a cash flow crisis that forced him to liquidate long-term investments at a significant loss. Proper liquidity layering would have prevented this situation by maintaining sufficient accessible capital for such contingencies.

The third principle is **income smoothing.** Unlike employees with predictable paychecks, entrepreneurs often experience irregular income with significant fluctuations throughout the year. Your investment approach needs to accommodate these patterns rather than assuming steady monthly contributions.

Effective income smoothing strategies include establishing a separate income stabilization account that collects business distributions during high-income periods and then releases steady monthly transfers to both living expenses and investment accounts. This creates consistency in your personal finances, despite business irregularities.

A seasonal business owner implemented this approach by directing all business distributions to a dedicated account during her high-revenue months. This account then transferred fixed amounts monthly to her household and investment accounts throughout the year, creating steady investment contributions despite her lumpy business income. This approach increased her annual investment contributions by over 40% compared to her previous reactive approach.

The fourth principle is **correlation management.** Most investment advisors focus on diversification across asset classes but fail to consider how these investments correlate with your business. As an entrepreneur, you need investments that don't move in the same direction as your company during economic changes.

Effective correlation management means understanding what economic factors affect your business and then selecting investments that respond differently to those same factors. For example, if your business thrives during inflationary periods, your personal investments might include assets that perform well during deflation or stable price environments.

A construction company owner recognized that his business performed best during economic booms when construction activity increased. He deliberately structured his personal investments to include certain bonds, defensive dividend stocks, and specialized alternative investments that historically performed well during economic slowdowns. This approach protected his overall wealth during industry cycles that temporarily reduced his business income.

The fifth principle is **tax integration.** Your investment strategy must work in harmony with your business tax planning rather than as a separate consideration. Investment decisions that make sense in isolation might create tax inefficiencies when considered alongside your business situation.

Effective tax integration includes coordinating investment activities with business income patterns, utilizing business entity structures to enhance investment tax efficiency, and timing investment transactions to complement business tax situations. This coordinated approach minimizes the total tax drag on your wealth-building.

The sixth principle is **opportunity reserve maintenance**. As an entrepreneur, you encounter business opportunities that require capital more frequently than employees do. Your investment strategy should include a dedicated opportunity reserve that remains available for business or investment situations with exceptional potential.

This reserve typically represents 5% to 15% of your investment portfolio held in accessible but productive assets. Unlike emergency funds that sit in cash, this reserve might be in liquid investments that generate returns while remaining accessible within weeks rather than months when compelling opportunities arise.

A business owner maintained a $200,000 opportunity reserve in a combination of ultra-short-term bond funds and cash equivalents. When a competitor unexpectedly offered to sell their client list at a steep discount during a cash crunch, the business owner accessed this reserve within days to make the purchase. This acquisition increased his business revenue by 30% and paid back the investment within seven months—an opportunity he would have missed without accessible capital.

The seventh principle is **psychological sustainability.** The most mathematically optimal investment strategy fails if it creates anxiety that prevents consistent implementation. As an entrepreneur, you need an investment approach that aligns with your psychological comfort, given the stress and uncertainty of running a business. David Booth, the founder of Dimensional Funds, has stated that the most important thing about an investment philosophy is that you have one you can stick with.[1]

Effective psychological sustainability might mean accepting slightly lower theoretical returns in exchange for an approach you'll maintain during business challenges. It often includes automating investment decisions to remove the emotional burden during stressful business periods when your decision-making capacity is already taxed.

---

1. David Booth, "Life, Invested: A collection of essays by David Booth" (PDF), Dimensional, vonborstel.com, July 2024, https://vonborstel.com/wp-content/uploads/2024/10/life-invested-a-collection-of-essays-by-david-booth-1.pdf.

One entrepreneur worked with her advisor to develop a theoretically optimal portfolio that maximized expected returns. But during a business crisis, she found herself unable to maintain the approach, making emotional decisions that significantly reduced her long-term results. She later adopted a slightly more conservative strategy with greater automation that produced better results because she maintained it consistently, even during business challenges.

The Wealthy Entrepreneur's Investment Framework recognizes that your situation differs fundamentally from typical employees' situations. Translation: If you want to build true wealth, you'd better have an entrepreneur-centric approach to investing.

By implementing these seven principles, you create an investment approach that complements your business and doesn't conflict with it. This integrated strategy builds personal wealth that provides true security regardless of business fluctuations.

Building Your Wealth Ecosystem

In this section, we will look at potential assets and portfolio designs. This is neither an investment recommendation nor investment advice. You should consult your own financial advisor prior to taking action.

Most business owners think about individual investments. Smart entrepreneurs build complete wealth ecosystems. A wealth ecosystem is a diverse collection of assets that work together to create financial security, growth, and eventually income without requiring your active involvement. It's not just about investing; it's about having the right mix of assets that complement each other and your business.

Your wealth ecosystem should include different types of assets that serve different purposes in your financial life. Some provide growth, others generate income, others offer tax advantages, and still others provide liquidity when needed. The right combination creates resilience against economic changes while building wealth in all conditions.

The first component of your ecosystem is **foundation assets**. These form the stable core of your personal wealth, providing security and liquidity. They typically include cash reserves, high-quality short-term bonds, and similar stable investments. While these assets won't produce spectacular returns, they create the secure foundation that allows you to take appropriate risks elsewhere.

Foundation assets may normally make up 5% to 15% of an established entrepreneur's external wealth ecosystem. In the early stages of a business, this percentage may be higher due to the need for more security, but it tends to decrease as overall wealth increases. The key is maintaining enough stability to weather business challenges without emotional decisions while not keeping too much capital in low-return vehicles.

One business owner maintained 40% of her personal investments in foundation assets despite having a stable, profitable business for over a decade. This excessive caution was costing her significant growth opportunities. After reducing her foundation assets to 15% and reallocating the difference to growth assets, she increased her portfolio returns by over 2% annually without creating unmanageable risk.

The second component is **growth assets.** These investments focus on long-term appreciation rather than current income. They typically include diversified stock investments, certain real estate holdings, and private equity opportunities. These assets provide the engine that grows your wealth over time through compound returns.

Growth assets should typically represent 40% to 60% of your wealth ecosystem, depending on your age, risk tolerance, and business stability. The specific mix in this category should complement your business exposure, not duplicate it. If your business is in technology, your growth assets might emphasize other sectors, like health care, consumer staples, or industrials, to create true diversification.

A manufacturing business owner had concentrated his growth assets in industrial stocks similar to his own company. When manufacturing faced industry-wide challenges, both his business and personal investments suffered simultaneously. After redistributing his growth assets across multiple uncorrelated sectors, his overall wealth became much more stable, despite ongoing business volatility.

The third component is **income assets**. These investments generate regular cash flow rather than focusing primarily on growth. They typically include dividend stocks, income-producing real estate, bonds, structured notes, and similar vehicles. These assets eventually provide the income stream that gives you financial independence from your business.

Income assets should typically start at 10% to 20% of your wealth ecosystem in early stages, then gradually increase as you approach your desired financial independence date. The allocation depends on how soon you want the option to step back from your business and how much income you need to support your lifestyle.

One entrepreneur maintained no income assets and focused entirely on growth. When health issues temporarily prevented him from running his business, he had no alternative income sources and faced financial stress despite substantial net worth. After rebuilding his portfolio to include 25% income assets, he created enough reliable cash flow to cover basic expenses regardless of business performance.

The fourth component is **tax-advantaged assets.** These investments utilize special account structures or tax treatments to minimize the tax drag on your wealth-building. They typically include qualified retirement accounts, certain insurance structures, real estate investments that benefit from depreciation, and opportunity zone investments.

Strategically integrate tax-advantaged assets throughout your wealth ecosystem rather than viewing them as a separate category. The percentage varies widely based on your tax situation, business structure, and available opportunities. The key is maximizing after-tax returns instead of pre-tax returns when making investment decisions.

A service business owner implemented this approach by directing a significant portion of her wealth-building through advanced retirement structures, including a cash balance plan. This allowed her to shield over $150,000 annually from current taxation while building wealth in tax-advantaged accounts. Over seven years, this approach created over $400,000 in tax savings that remained in her wealth ecosystem rather than going to tax authorities.

The fifth component is **opportunity assets**. These investments offer higher potential returns in exchange for less liquidity, more complexity, or greater risk. They typically include private company investments, specialized real estate projects, venture capital, or other alternative investments not available to most retail investors.

Opportunity assets should typically represent 5% to 20% of your wealth ecosystem once your foundation is established. This allocation allows you to capture exceptional returns from special situations while limiting the impact of inevitable losses in this higher-risk category. The opportunities should leverage your unique knowledge, network, and capabilities as an entrepreneur.

One technology entrepreneur allocated 15% of his wealth ecosystem to early-stage investments in his industry, where his specialized knowledge provided a competitive advantage. While several investments failed completely, two produced returns exceeding ten times his initial investment. Despite the failures, this portion of his portfolio outperformed traditional investments by more than three times overall, significantly accelerating his wealth-building.

The sixth component is **legacy assets.** These investments focus on multigenerational wealth transfer rather than current returns. They typically include specialized trust structures. Permanent life insurance, family limited partnerships, and similar financial vehicles are designed to efficiently transfer wealth to future generations or charitable causes.

Legacy assets become increasingly important as your wealth ecosystem grows beyond your personal needs. The allocation depends on your family situation and wealth transfer goals. The key is implementing these structures early enough to maximize their long-term benefits while maintaining sufficient assets for your own financial security.

A business owner with substantial wealth implemented a legacy asset strategy that included specialized insurance structures and dynasty trusts. This approach created over $5 million in projected tax savings for wealth transfers to his children compared to traditional inheritance methods. By implementing these structures while still in his forties, he maximized their long-term impact while maintaining complete financial control during his lifetime.

Building your complete wealth ecosystem requires integrating these components into a cohesive strategy rather than viewing them as separate investments. The optimal allocation across categories evolves as your business matures, your wealth grows, and your personal goals change. Regular ecosystem reviews keep your asset mix aligned with your current situation rather than reflecting past circumstances.

The entrepreneurs who build complete wealth ecosystems create financial resilience that endures through business cycles, economic changes, and personal life transitions. Their wealth continues growing even when business challenges arise, creating true financial independence that doesn't depend on constant business success.

The Seventy-Two-Hour Liquidity Rule

Entrepreneurs face unique financial risks. Business opportunities and threats emerge with little warning. Markets shift overnight. Clients delay payments unexpectedly. The Seventy-Two-Hour Liquidity Rule addresses these realities by making sure you can access critical capital within three days, regardless of what happens in your business or the broader economy.

This rule states that entrepreneurs should maintain enough accessible capital to cover three needs within seventy-two hours: business emergency funding, personal financial obligations, and unexpected opportunities. The exact amount varies based on your situation, but the principle remains constant—certain capital must remain accessible within three days without significant penalties or losses.

Most entrepreneurs violate this rule in one of two ways. Some keep too little accessible capital, investing everything for maximum growth or pouring all available funds back into their business. Others keep too much in cash, earning minimal returns due to fear of being caught short. The Seventy-Two-Hour Liquidity Rule provides a balanced framework that protects against emergencies while still allowing most capital to seek appropriate returns.

The first component of the rule is your business bridge fund. This is capital you can access quickly to address unexpected business needs without disrupting operations or growth initiatives. The appropriate size typically ranges from 5% to 15% of annual business revenue, depending on your industry volatility, payment cycles, and fixed cost structure.

This fund should be separate from regular business operating accounts so it can't be used for routine expenses. It typically belongs on your personal balance sheet rather than your business balance sheet, creating clear separation while remaining accessible when needed. The structure might include a combination of high-yield savings accounts, ultra-short-term bond funds, or similar vehicles that provide some return while maintaining accessibility.

One service business owner maintained no business bridge fund, keeping minimal cash in the company and withdrawing all excess profit monthly. When three major clients simultaneously delayed payments during an economic downturn, he faced a cash crisis that forced expensive emergency financing. After implementing a business bridge fund equal to 10% of annual revenue, he navigated subsequent payment delays without disruption or additional costs.

The second component is your personal safety reserve. This is capital you can access quickly to cover personal financial obligations during business disruptions. The appropriate size typically ranges from three to six months of personal expenses, depending on your business stability, other income sources, and family obligations.

This reserve should be separate from both business accounts and regular personal checking accounts so it can't be used for nonemergency purposes. It typically belongs in high-yield savings accounts, money market funds, or similar vehicles that provide some return while remaining immediately accessible. The key is maintaining this reserve regardless of business performance rather than building it only when convenient.

A business owner with inconsistent cash flow maintained no personal safety reserve, covering household expenses directly from business distributions. When business challenges temporarily reduced distributions, he faced personal financial stress despite significant business assets. After he established a personal safety reserve covering four months of household expenses, subsequent business fluctuations caused no disruption to his family's financial stability.

The third component is your opportunity fund. This is capital you can deploy quickly when unexpected business or investment opportunities arise. The appropriate size typically ranges from 5% to 10% of your personal net worth outside the business, depending on your industry, network, and typical opportunity size.

This fund should be more productive than pure cash but remain accessible within seventy-two hours without significant penalties. It typically belongs in ultra-short-term bond funds, conservative balanced funds with redemption guarantees, or similar vehicles that generate meaningful returns while maintaining necessary liquidity. The key is having this capital ready before opportunities appear rather than scrambling to liquidate other investments when time is critical.

One entrepreneur maintained his entire portfolio in long-term investments, requiring weeks for proper liquidation. When a competitor unexpectedly offered their business for sale at a significant discount during a cash crisis, he couldn't move quickly enough to secure the deal. After establishing an opportunity fund equal to 7% of his net worth, he successfully acquired two smaller competitors during subsequent industry consolidation, significantly increasing his market share.

The Seventy-Two-Hour Liquidity Rule requires regular rebalancing as your business and personal finances evolve. As your business stabilizes, you might reduce your business bridge fund percentage while maintaining the absolute dollar amount. As your wealth grows, your opportunity fund should increase proportionally to match the size of potential opportunities in your network and industry.

Implementing this rule doesn't mean keeping excessive cash that earns nothing. It means strategically positioning specific portions of your capital in vehicles that balance accessibility with reasonable returns. The goal is to maintain necessary liquidity while still allowing most of your wealth to pursue appropriate growth in less liquid investments.

The entrepreneurs who follow the Seventy-Two-Hour Liquidity Rule sleep better during business challenges while still capturing opportunities others miss. They maintain emotional stability during market volatility because they know their immediate needs are covered, regardless of temporary disruptions. Most importantly, they make better long-term investment decisions because short-term liquidity needs don't force them to prematurely liquidate growth assets.

One business owner implemented the complete Seventy-Two-Hour Liquidity Rule with 8% of annual revenue in his business bridge fund, four months of expenses in his personal safety reserve, and 6% of net worth in his opportunity fund. When the COVID pandemic created both business challenges and unique acquisition opportunities, he maintained operations without stress while purchasing a struggling competitor at a significant discount. This balanced liquidity approach protected his existing business while enabling growth that competitors couldn't pursue due to their liquidity constraints.

Chapter 5 Recap: Activating Your Personal Wealth Engine

You now understand the critical components of your Personal Wealth Engine—the system that transforms business success into lasting personal fortune. Throughout this chapter, we've explored how to build wealth outside your business that grows independently, provides true security, and eventually creates financial freedom regardless of your company's performance.

Key Insights

Personal Wealth Engine Goals

- Build wealth outside your business that grows independently and provides true financial security.
- Create resilience against business challenges or economic disruptions.
- Achieve financial freedom regardless of your company's performance.

Importance of Your Personal Balance Sheet

- Tools for assessing and growing your wealth outside the business:
  - **Wealth Ratio**: Personal net worth (excluding business) ÷ business value.
  - **Personal Balance Sheet Growth Plan**: A strategy to accumulate diverse assets.
  - **Wealth Freedom Number**: The amount of wealth required to achieve financial independence.
  - **Balance Sheet Protection**: Safeguards to prevent over-concentration of finances.

Wealthy Entrepreneur's Investment Framework

- Designed specifically for business owners:
  - **Risk Balancing**: Manage risk across business and personal investments.
  - **Liquidity Layering**: Maintain accessible funds for emergencies and opportunities.

- **Income Smoothing**: Ensure steady cash flow through investments.
- **Correlation Management**: Avoid over-reliance on correlated assets.
- **Tax Integration**: Minimize tax drag across investments.
- **Opportunity Reserve**: Allocate funds for high-return opportunities.
- **Psychological Sustainability**: Align investments with your comfort level to stay consistent.

The Wealth Ecosystem

- Six key asset categories to diversify and strengthen your finances:
    - **Foundation Assets**: Stability and security (e.g., cash reserves).
    - **Growth Assets**: Long-term appreciation (e.g., stocks, real estate).
    - **Income Assets**: Generate consistent cash flow (e.g., rental properties, dividends).
    - **Tax-Advantaged Assets**: Reduce tax burden (e.g., retirement accounts).
    - **Opportunity Assets**: Capture exceptional returns (e.g., venture capital).
    - **Legacy Assets**: Facilitate wealth transfer (e.g., trusts, estates).

The Seventy-Two-Hour Liquidity Rule

- Ensure access to critical capital within three days:
    - **Business Bridge Fund**: Covers unexpected company needs.
    - **Personal Safety Reserve**: Ensures household stability.
    - **Opportunity Fund**: Ready capital for time-sensitive investments.

Action Steps

1. Calculate Your Wealth Ratio

- Divide your personal net worth (excluding business assets) by your business value.
- Use this as a baseline to measure your progress in transferring business success to personal wealth.

2. Determine Your Ideal Asset Allocation

- Based on the **Wealth Ecosystem Framework**, decide what percentage of your investments should go into:
    - Foundation, growth, income, tax-advantaged, opportunity, and legacy assets.
    - Tailor the allocation to your business stage, risk tolerance, and financial goals.

3. Identify Liquidity Gaps

- Compare current accessible capital against the **Seventy-Two-Hour Liquidity Rule**:
  - Calculate how much you need in your business bridge fund, personal safety reserve, and opportunity fund.
  - Identify how much additional capital is required to close these gaps.

4. Schedule Your First Wealth Transfer

- Plan your initial transfer of funds from business to personal accounts:
  - Decide the amount to transfer.
  - Select which investments will receive these funds based on your allocation plan.
  - Establish this as a recurring process to activate and sustain your wealth engine.

Key Takeaways for Transformation

- **Wealth Beyond Business**: Build assets that grow independently of your business efforts.
- **Resilience and Security**: Protect yourself from business challenges and economic downturns.
- **Systematic Transfers**: Continuously move a portion of your business profits to personal wealth assets.

Next Steps in the Book

- Learn advanced strategies for scaling your wealth ecosystem.
- Explore ways to align your wealth-building efforts with long-term legacy planning.
- Discover how to integrate risk management into your personal wealth engine.

Chapter 6

The Financial Ecosystem Integration Framework

The Coordination Problem

You have a CPA who handles your taxes. A financial advisor manages your investments. Your lawyer set up your business structure years ago. Your insurance agent sold you some policies. And you have a bookkeeper or maybe even a fractional CFO helping with business finances. Each of these professionals is smart and well-intentioned. But they all work separately, rarely talking to each other and often giving you conflicting advice. This coordination issue is causing you significant financial losses.

Most entrepreneurs don't realize how much wealth they're losing through this fragmented approach. When your advisors don't coordinate, each optimizes their own small piece of your financial picture without seeing how it affects the whole. Your CPA, if they suggest tax strategies, creates problems for your investment plan. Your financial advisor recommends moves that increase your tax bill. Your attorney sets up structures that make financing harder to obtain. And you're stuck in the middle, trying to make sense of it all.

I recently worked with a gentleman who owns a $2 million coaching practice. He had five different financial professionals advising him—none of whom ever spoke to each other. His CPA had him structured as an S corporation to avoid self-employment tax. Meanwhile, his financial advisor had him maxing out a SEP IRA, not realizing that with his business structure, he could have used a solo 401(k) that would allow three times the annual contribution. This single coordination failure had cost him over $400,000 in lost retirement savings over seven years.

The coordination problem creates three major wealth-destroying gaps. First, strategy conflicts occur when one advisor recommends something that undermines another advisor's plan. Second, you can miss opportunities when no single advisor sees the complete picture needed to identify your best moves. Third, implementation failures occur when good advice gets lost in the handoff between professionals who don't communicate effectively.

These gaps compound over time. A strategy conflict that costs you $20,000 this year doesn't just cost you $20,000. It costs you that amount plus all the future growth that money could have generated. Over twenty years at 8% growth, that single $20,000 mistake compounds to over $93,000 in lost wealth. Now multiply that by the dozens of uncoordinated decisions made across your financial life each year.

The problem gets worse as you become more successful. When you were starting out, maybe you just had a simple tax return and a small retirement account. Coordination wasn't as critical. But as your business grows and your financial life becomes more complex, the cost of poor coordination grows exponentially. More money flows through more accounts with more tax implications and more planning opportunities—all of which require more coordination to optimize.

Most financial professionals aren't trained to solve this problem. They specialize in their narrow area of expertise and rarely see beyond it. Your CPA excels at tax compliance but may know little about investment strategies. Your financial advisor understands markets but may have limited knowledge of business entity structures. Your attorney drafts excellent legal documents but may not understand their tax implications. None of them are incentivized to coordinate with the others.

Even when these professionals try to coordinate, they often speak different languages. Tax professionals talk about code sections and deduction strategies. Investment advisors discuss asset allocation and risk-adjusted returns. Bookkeepers and accountants focus on data that has happened in the past, with little ability to forecast and predict the future. Attorneys focus on liability protection and governance structures. Without someone translating between these specialized vocabularies, critical details get lost and opportunities slip through the cracks.

The coordination problem also creates a significant burden for you. Without a structured system for integrating advisors, you become the reluctant quarterback and the bottleneck of your financial team. You spend valuable time in meetings, explaining what another advisor recommended, trying to reconcile conflicting advice, and making decisions you don't feel fully qualified to make. This cognitive and emotional burden takes a toll beyond the direct financial costs.

Solving the coordination problem requires more than just introducing your advisors to each other or having occasional group meetings. It demands a systematic framework for integration—a structured approach that keeps everyone working toward your overall wealth objectives rather than optimizing their individual pieces of the puzzle. This framework must include clear communication protocols, regular coordination meetings, centralized sharing of information, and a designated integration leader who maintains the big-picture view. We believe that the best way to integrate your financial ecosystem is with a chief wealth officer.

Building Your Wealth Advisory Team

A chief wealth officer leading the right advisory team can dramatically accelerate your wealth-building. The wrong team can cost you millions in missed opportunities, unnecessary taxes, and poor investment returns. Yet most entrepreneurs select advisors haphazardly based on convenience, personal referrals, or whoever they happen to meet first. This random approach virtually guarantees coordination problems and wealth-destroying gaps.

Building an effective wealth advisory team starts with understanding the key roles needed for entrepreneurial wealth creation. Unlike employees, who might need only a tax preparer and basic financial advisor, entrepreneurs require specialized expertise across multiple domains. Your core team typically includes a tax strategist (not just a tax preparer); a wealth advisor (not just an investment manager); legal counsel focused on business and wealth structures; and a business financial specialist, like a CFO and bookkeeper.

Many founders ask, "Which role is most important?"

The answer is all of them. It's the sum of the entire team, coordinated and working together, that creates the magic. Many people misunderstand the roles in an entrepreneur's financial ecosystem. The tax strategist's role is perhaps the most misunderstood. Most entrepreneurs use CPAs, who excel at compliance—accurately filing required forms and keeping their clients out of trouble. But wealth-building entrepreneurs need tax strategists who proactively identify opportunities, coordinate with other advisors, and implement multiyear tax optimization plans. The difference between these approaches can easily amount to $50,000 to $250,000 annually for successful business owners.

When evaluating potential tax strategists, look for a professional who primarily serves business owners in your revenue range, discusses tax planning in the context of your overall wealth objectives (not just this year's return), and proactively contacts you throughout the year (not just at tax time). Avoid professionals who serve mainly employees, focus exclusively on compliance, or wait for you to call them with questions.

One business owner switched from a traditional CPA to a specialized tax strategist who worked exclusively with entrepreneurs. The new advisor immediately identified five strategies the previous accountant had missed, creating over $83,000 in tax savings the first year while better supporting the owner's wealth-building goals. The strategies weren't aggressive or risky. They were simply approaches that required business expertise the previous CPA lacked.

The wealth advisor role requires similar specialization. Most financial advisors build their practices serving employees and retirees with stable incomes and simple financial lives. They lack the expertise to address the unique challenges entrepreneurs face: irregular income streams, concentrated business risk, complex entity structures, and the need to coordinate business and personal finances as an integrated system.

When selecting a wealth advisor, look for a professional who specializes in serving entrepreneur business owners, understands business financial statements and valuation methods, and can articulate how their investment approach complements your business risk profile. Avoid advisors who primarily serve employees, focus exclusively on investment products, or don't ask detailed questions about your business structure and strategy.

A technology company owner replaced his traditional financial advisor with one specializing in entrepreneurial wealth strategies. The new advisor immediately restructured his portfolio to complement rather than duplicate his business risk exposure and coordinated with his tax strategist to implement more efficient wealth transfer methods. These changes increased his after-tax returns by over 3.2% annually while reducing overall risk—a difference that would create hundreds of thousands in additional wealth over a decade.

The legal counsel role for wealth-building entrepreneurs goes far beyond basic business formation. You need an attorney who understands how legal structures affect both business operations and personal wealth-building. This professional helps create entity structures that support tax efficiency, asset protection, and eventual wealth transfer or business exit. They ensure that your legal foundation supports rather than hinders your overall wealth strategy.

When evaluating legal counsel, look for an attorney who regularly works with entrepreneurs in your revenue range, coordinates with your tax and financial advisors before making recommendations, and can clearly explain how their suggested structures support your wealth objectives. Steer clear of attorneys who offer universal entity recommendations, concentrate solely on liability protection without taking into account tax implications, or infrequently refresh their understanding of evolving laws impacting business owners.

A service business owner engaged a specialized business attorney to review the legal structures her previous lawyer had created years earlier. The new attorney identified that her existing structure created significant tax inefficiencies and barriers to wealth transfer. By restructuring her entities in coordination with her tax strategist, she reduced her annual tax burden by over $47,000 while creating a clear pathway for eventually transferring the business to her children.

The chief wealth officer is a specialist role that provides the foundation for all wealth decisions by giving you accurate, timely financial information about your company and your personal wealth accumulation goals. They help translate business performance into personal wealth-building opportunities by maintaining clear financial aspirations, records, and projections.

When selecting this team member, look for a professional who understands how business finances connect to personal wealth-building, provides forward-looking projections (not just historical statements), and communicates in terms you can easily understand and act upon. Avoid specialists who focus exclusively on compliance or historical reporting, can't explain how business decisions affect your personal finances, or speak in technical jargon that obscures rather than clarifies your financial position.

One business owner upgraded from a basic bookkeeper to a CWO with wealth-building expertise. The new advisor implemented cash flow forecasting that identified opportunities to increase owner distributions by 40% without affecting business operations. This single change accelerated personal wealth-building dramatically while providing greater clarity for decision-making.

Beyond selecting the right individual advisors, you need to establish clear coordination protocols. Each team member should understand their role in your overall wealth strategy, know when and how to communicate with other advisors, and recognize which decisions require cross-functional input. These protocols prevent the strategy conflicts and missed opportunities that plague most entrepreneurs' financial lives.

The most effective advisory teams operate with a designated quarterback who maintains the big-picture view and ensures coordination. The chief wealth officer, with their holistic approach, is going to oversee the entire financial ecosystem. A designated integration leader dramatically improves team effectiveness by creating clear accountability for coordination.

Building your wealth advisory team isn't about finding the cheapest professionals or those with the most impressive credentials. It's about creating a coordinated group of specialists who understand entrepreneurial wealth creation and work together toward your objectives. The right team more than pays for itself through tax savings, improved investment returns, and captured opportunities that a fragmented approach would miss.

The Quarterly Wealth Alignment Meeting

Most entrepreneurs meet with their financial advisors separately at different times and discuss different aspects of their finances. This fragmented approach virtually guarantees coordination failures. A quarterly wealth alignment meeting solves this problem by regularly bringing your key advisors together so that everyone is working toward your wealth objectives rather than their individual agendas.

This structured meeting isn't just about getting everyone in the same room (or on the same video call). It follows a format designed to identify opportunities, resolve conflicts, and create accountability for implementation. When properly conducted, these quarterly meetings prevent strategy gaps and missed opportunities.

The first step is determining who should attend. Your core participants typically include your tax strategist, your wealth advisor, and you. Depending on current priorities, you might also include your business attorney, insurance specialist, estate planning attorney, or business financial specialist. The key is involving the right professionals for the wealth objectives you're currently pursuing rather than automatically including everyone who plays any role in your finances.

One business owner initially tried to include seven different advisors in his alignment meetings. The sessions became unwieldy, with too many voices and not enough focus. When he streamlined the attendees to include a chief wealth officer, with others joining only for relevant agenda items, the meetings became far more productive. This focused approach identified and implemented strategies that had been lost in the previous information overload.

The second step is establishing a clear meeting structure. Effective wealth alignment meetings typically follow a consistent format:

1. **Business update:** Reviewing recent business performance and upcoming changes that might affect your wealth strategy
2. **Strategy review:** Examining progress on previously identified wealth-building opportunities
3. **Coordination issues:** Addressing any conflicts between recommendations from different advisors
4. **New opportunities:** Identifying new strategies based on current business and personal circumstances
5. **Implementation plan:** Assigning action items with deadlines and responsibilities.

This structured approach ensures that the meeting produces tangible results rather than becoming a general discussion that leads nowhere. Each section has a specific purpose in preventing the coordination problems that reduce wealth-building efficiency.

A technology company owner implemented this exact meeting structure with her advisory team. In their first session, they identified three coordination issues that had been silently undermining her wealth-building: her tax strategy conflicted with her investment approach, her business entity structure limited her retirement options, and her insurance coverage created unnecessary tax consequences. Resolving these conflicts through the structured meeting format added over $35,000 annually to her wealth-building capacity without requiring any new strategies—just better coordination of existing ones.

The third step is preparation and documentation. Each participant should receive an agenda and preparation guidelines at least one week before the meeting. They should come prepared with updates, recommendations, and questions relevant to current wealth objectives. During the meeting, someone should document all decisions, action items, and responsible parties. After the meeting, this documentation should be distributed to all participants for clear accountability.

Without this preparation and documentation, wealth alignment meetings often become unproductive conversations that don't lead to implemented strategies. The documentation creates a record of decisions that prevents the "I thought someone else was handling that" problem that frequently delays wealth-building actions.

One business owner had been holding occasional advisor meetings for years but saw little improvement in coordination. Once the advisors started preparing properly and tracking detailed action items, they identified and implemented strategies they had previously overlooked. The difference wasn't the advisors' capabilities. It was the structured approach that held them accountable for following through.

The fourth step is maintaining a system for tracking opportunities. Each wealth-building strategy identified during alignment meetings should be recorded in a central system that tracks its status, required actions, responsible parties, and expected benefits. With this system, which you review at each quarterly meeting, valuable opportunities don't get lost amid day-to-day business demands.

Many entrepreneurs identify good wealth-building strategies but never fully implement them because the actions get lost among competing priorities. This tracking system prevents this loss by maintaining visibility and accountability for each strategy between quarterly meetings.

An owner of a manufacturing company used a straightforward spreadsheet to put into practice fourteen wealth-building tactics that were discovered during alignment meetings. This visibility tool increased his implementation rate from approximately 30% to over 80% and captured an additional $120,000 annually in tax savings and investment improvements that would have otherwise been lost to incomplete execution. The strategies themselves weren't new, but implementing them created substantial wealth that had previously been left on the table.

The fifth step is establishing clear communication protocols between quarterly meetings. Your advisors need guidelines for when to consult each other directly rather than waiting for the next alignment meeting. These protocols typically specify which types of decisions require cross-functional input and which professionals should be consulted for different categories of financial moves.

Without these protocols, advisors often make recommendations in isolation that create problems in other areas of your financial life. Clear communication guidelines prevent these coordination failures between formal meetings.

One business owner established a simple rule: Any tax or investment decision involving more than $25,000 required consultation with her CWO before implementation. This single protocol prevented several potential conflicts, including an investment move that would have created over $30,000 in unnecessary taxes and a business structure change that would have limited investment options. These coordination benefits materialized between quarterly meetings because the communication protocols enabled ongoing alignment.

A fragmented advisory approach would miss five to ten significant wealth-building opportunities annually. But the quarterly wealth alignment meeting system typically identifies them. For successful entrepreneurs, these opportunities often represent $50,000 to $250,000 or more in annual wealth-building impact through reduced taxes, improved investment returns, captured business opportunities, and eliminated inefficiencies.

Beyond the direct financial benefits, this system dramatically reduces the burden of managing multiple advisors. Rather than serving as your financial team's reluctant quarterback, you establish a structure where coordination happens systematically with clear accountability. This reduces the cognitive and emotional load of wealth management, freeing your attention for business growth and personal priorities. We call this "emotional ROI." Let's face it—running a business can be overwhelming. Uncertainty and the weight of financial decisions can cause significant stress. The proper financial ecosystem, led by a holistic chief wealth officer, can help remove that burden. The goal is a clear plan, actionable insights, and someone to help you navigate challenges.

Becoming the CEO of Your Financial Life

Most entrepreneurs excel at running their businesses but struggle with their personal finances. They may learn to make confident, data-driven decisions in their companies but approach their wealth-building reactively, often abdicating responsibility to various advisors. This situation creates a dangerous gap between business success and personal financial security. Becoming the CEO of your financial life closes this gap by applying the same leadership principles to your wealth that you use in your business.

Being the financial CEO doesn't mean doing everything yourself or becoming an expert in taxes, investments, and legal structures. Just as in your business, effective leadership means setting clear objectives, assembling the right team, establishing accountability systems, and maintaining appropriate oversight. It means taking ultimate responsibility for results while delegating implementation to qualified specialists. We believe working with a chief wealth officer is ideal.

The first principle of financial CEO leadership is to have strategic clarity. You need a clear wealth strategy that defines objectives, time frames, and metrics for success. This strategy should align with your business goals and personal priorities rather than consisting of disconnected financial moves. It becomes the guiding document that your CWO uses and against which all advisor recommendations are evaluated.

Most entrepreneurs lack this strategic clarity. They make financial decisions reactively based on the advisor who spoke to them most recently or the article they just read. This scattered approach creates inconsistent results and missed opportunities. A clear wealth strategy provides the foundation for coordinated action across all financial domains.

One business owner created a one-page wealth strategy document outlining his objectives: building $3 million in assets outside his business within five years, reducing his tax rate to below 25%, creating college funds of $150,000 for each child, and establishing business succession options by age fifty-five. This clarity transformed his advisory relationships. Instead of bringing him random ideas, his CWO began presenting coordinated recommendations designed to achieve these stated objectives.

The second principle is to have mastery over information. Effective CEOs maintain dashboards that show key business metrics. Your financial life needs the same approach—a simple dashboard showing critical wealth metrics that you review regularly. This doesn't mean tracking every investment or reviewing complex reports. It means monitoring the five to seven key indicators that matter for your wealth objectives.

These indicators typically include your Wealth Ratio (personal assets divided by business value), Wealth Freedom Number progress (assets needed for financial independence), tax efficiency rate (taxes paid as a percentage of total income), wealth transfer rate (money moving from business to personal assets), and investment performance relative to appropriate benchmarks. Tracking these metrics creates awareness and accountability that drive better decisions.

A service business owner implemented a monthly financial dashboard tracking five key wealth metrics. This simple tool revealed that while her business was growing impressively, her personal wealth was increasing at less than half the rate it should have based on her income. This awareness prompted changes in her wealth transfer system that doubled the growth rate of her personal assets within six months while maintaining appropriate business investment.

The third principle is to provide clarity regarding who makes decisions. In your business, you clearly define who can make which decisions at what spending levels. Your wealth-building system needs the same clarity about which financial moves require your direct approval, which moves your advisors can implement independently, and which decisions require consultation among multiple professionals before proceeding.

Without this clarity, entrepreneurs often become bottlenecks in their own wealth-building. Some try to approve every minor decision, delaying implementation. Others abdicate too completely, allowing advisors to make major moves without proper oversight. Clear decision rights create the right balance between delegation and control.

One entrepreneur established a simple decision rights framework: Changes affecting less than $10,000 could be implemented by individual advisors within their domains; changes between $10,000 and $50,000 required notification before implementation; and changes above $50,000 required his direct approval. This clarity accelerated smaller implementations while ensuring that he maintained control of major financial moves. The system prevented both micromanagement and excessive abdication.

The fourth principle is to establish accountability. Business CEOs establish clear metrics and regular review processes to guarantee performance. Your wealth-building requires the same discipline to regularly review progress with the chief wealth officer and systematically evaluate results against objectives. This accountability prevents the drift and incomplete implementation that plague most entrepreneurial finances.

Effective accountability, coordinated and led by your chief wealth officer, includes quarterly performance reviews with each key advisor, annual comprehensive strategy assessments, and metrics for measuring advisor value. These systems keep your financial professionals focused on your objectives rather than their own agendas or standard procedures.

A technology company owner implemented quarterly accountability reviews with each financial advisor. These structured evaluations measured progress against specific wealth objectives rather than generic benchmarks. When one advisor consistently failed to meet implementation commitments despite repeated feedback, the owner replaced them with a professional more aligned with his wealth-building approach. This accountability dramatically improved his overall financial results by making sure each team member delivered on their commitments.

The fifth principle is to continuously learn without overreacting. Business CEOs stay informed about industry trends without chasing every new idea. Your wealth-building requires the same balanced approach—remaining educated about financial strategies without constantly changing direction based on the latest article or podcast. This measured learning prevents both stagnation and scattered implementation.

Effective financial CEOs establish learning routines focused on their current wealth priorities. They might read one relevant book quarterly, attend two educational events annually, and schedule periodic strategy sessions with advisors to explore new approaches. This structured learning creates improvement without distraction.

One business owner had been changing investment approaches every few months based on various articles and recommendations, creating poor results and unnecessary taxes. After implementing a structured learning system focused on his wealth stage, he developed a consistent strategy that he maintained with periodic refinements rather than wholesale changes. This stability improved his investment returns by over 4% annually compared to his previous scattered approach.

The sixth principle is to integrate leadership. Business CEOs ensure that different departments work together toward company objectives. Your wealth-building requires the same integration. Someone must maintain the big picture and keep all financial domains working together. As the CEO of your financial life, you establish the structures that create this integration, even if you delegate the technical implementation.

This integration leadership includes the quarterly wealth alignment meetings discussed earlier, clear communication protocols among advisors, and regular review of how strategies in one area affect other financial domains. These integration mechanisms prevent the coordination failures that reduce wealth-building efficiency.

A professional services firm owner implemented comprehensive integration leadership across her financial life. She established quarterly alignment meetings, clear communication protocols, and regular cross-domain reviews. This systematic approach identified over $95,000 in annual tax savings and investment improvements that had been missed when her advisors worked in isolation. The strategies themselves weren't new or complex—they simply required proper integration to identify and implement them.

Becoming the CEO of your financial life transforms your relationship with money. Instead of feeling overwhelmed by complexity or disconnected from your own finances, you establish the same confident leadership that drives your business success. This leadership creates the bridge between business profit and personal wealth that most entrepreneurs never build.

Entrepreneurs who implement these financial CEO principles typically see 15% to 40% improvements in their wealth-building results without changing their business performance or income. The difference comes not from working harder or earning more but from applying effective leadership to their personal finances. They create true financial security by systematically translating business success into personal wealth through coordinated, strategic implementation.

Chapter 6 Recap: Integrating Your Financial Ecosystem

You now understand the critical importance of integration across your financial ecosystem. Throughout this chapter, we've explored how to transform a fragmented collection of advisors into a coordinated team that works toward your wealth objectives. Let's recap the key insights and outline your immediate action steps.

Key Insights

The Coordination Problem

- Fragmented financial advice from uncoordinated advisors leads to:
  1. Strategy conflicts.
  2. Missed opportunities.
  3. Implementation failures.
- Many entrepreneurs feel confusion and inefficiency despite having multiple advisors.

Building Your Wealth Advisory Team

- Assemble specialists who understand entrepreneurial wealth creation:
  1. Chief Wealth Officer (CWO): A team leader who ensures coordination and alignment.
  2. Tax Strategist: Proactively plans, rather than just preparing returns.
  3. Wealth Advisor: Focuses on business owners, not just traditional investments.
  4. Legal Counsel: Designs wealth-supporting structures.
  5. Business Financial Specialists: Connect company performance with personal wealth-building strategies.

The Quarterly Wealth Alignment Meeting System

- A structured approach to regularly bringing advisors together:
  1. Share business updates and refine strategy.
  2. Resolve conflicts between advisors' recommendations.
  3. Identify new opportunities and ensure smooth implementation.
- Prevents gaps and conflicts caused by advisors working in isolation.

Becoming the CEO of Your Financial Life

- Apply business leadership principles to your wealth-building:
  1. Clarify Strategy: Define clear objectives and timelines.
  2. Master Information: Track key financial metrics.
  3. Clarify Decision Rights: Balance delegation and control.
  4. Create Accountability: Ensure advisors deliver results.
  5. Continuous Learning: Stay informed without overreacting.
  6. Integrated Leadership: Maintain a big-picture view of your wealth ecosystem.

Action Steps

1. Map Your Current Advisory Relationships

- Create a diagram of your current advisors, their roles, and how often they communicate.
- Look for gaps and overlaps that reduce efficiency and create confusion.

2. Schedule Your First Wealth Alignment Meeting

- Identify 2-3 critical advisors for your current priorities.
- Set a 90-minute meeting within 30 days using the structured agenda from this chapter.
- Ask each advisor to prepare updates and recommendations.
- This meeting often uncovers immediate opportunities worth significant value.

3. Create Your Wealth Strategy Document

- Develop a one-page document outlining:
  - Financial objectives.
  - Timelines.
  - Metrics for success.
- Share this document with all advisors to ensure alignment and unified decision-making.

4. Establish Your Financial CEO Dashboard

- Identify 5-7 key metrics to track, such as:
  - Wealth Ratio.
  - Progress toward Wealth Freedom Number.
  - Tax efficiency rate.
  - Wealth transfer rate.
  - Investment performance benchmarks.
- Create a system to update and review these metrics monthly to maintain oversight and accountability.

Key Takeaways for Transformation

- Integration Wins: Coordinated advisors dramatically improve wealth-building results.
- Leadership is Key: You are the CEO of your financial life, responsible for ensuring alignment and strategy.
- Unlock Efficiency: Entrepreneurs who integrate their financial ecosystem capture 15%-40% more wealth-building value from the same income and advisors.

Next Steps in the Book

- Learn how to scale and refine this system as your wealth grows.
- Discover advanced strategies for legacy planning and risk management.
- Explore methods for simplifying wealth management without losing control.

By implementing the Financial Ecosystem Integration Framework, you ensure that all components of your wealth-building system work seamlessly together. This final piece completes the transformation from fragmented financial advice to a coordinated strategy that powers your journey to financial independence.

Chapter 7

From Revenue to Freedom: Your Wealth Independence Plan

Calculating Your Wealth Freedom Number

Most entrepreneurs have no idea how much money they need to become financially free. They work hard building businesses but never stop to calculate the exact amount of wealth required for true financial independence. This missing number—your Wealth Freedom Number—is the most important figure in your entire wealth plan, yet most business owners can't tell you what it is.

Your Wealth Freedom Number represents the amount of wealth you need outside your business to maintain your desired lifestyle without working. It's the point where your passive income from investments exceeds your expenses, making work optional. Without this precise target, you're essentially building wealth blindfolded, hoping you'll eventually have enough without knowing what "enough" means.

Calculating your Wealth Freedom Number starts with understanding your true lifestyle costs. Most entrepreneurs drastically underestimate what they spend. They think about their mortgage, car payments, and basic bills but forget dozens of expenses that flow through their business or happen irregularly. This leads to Wealth Freedom Numbers that are far too low, creating dangerous financial gaps.

To find your lifestyle cost, track all personal expenses for three months. Include everything: housing, transportation, food, entertainment, travel, health care, children's activities, subscriptions, personal care, gifts, and occasional large purchases averaged monthly. Don't forget to consider expenses that are currently covered by your business but would become personal if you stepped away, such as cell phones, vehicles, travel, technology, entertainment, and health insurance.

One business owner thought her monthly expenses were about $12,000. After proper tracking, she discovered her true lifestyle cost was over $22,000 when including everything currently flowing through her business. This single realization almost doubled her Wealth Freedom Number, entirely changing her Wealth Timeline and strategy.

Next, adjust this monthly figure for future changes. Will your mortgage eventually disappear? Do you plan to travel more? Will health care costs increase? Will children's expenses change? Make realistic adjustments for how your lifestyle might evolve. This isn't about cutting costs—it's about accurately projecting what financial independence means for you.

Now multiply your adjusted monthly expense by 12 to get your annual lifestyle cost. For most entrepreneurs, this ranges from $150,000 to $500,000, depending on location, family size, and personal preferences. There's no right or wrong number—just your number based on the life you want to live.

To calculate your base Wealth Freedom Number, multiply your annual lifestyle cost by 25. This uses the widely accepted 4% safe withdrawal rate, meaning you can sustainably withdraw 4% of your investment portfolio annually without depleting it over time. For example, if your annual lifestyle cost is $200,000, your base Wealth Freedom Number is $5,000,000 ($200,000 × 25).

This base calculation assumes all your wealth is in traditional investment portfolios. But many entrepreneurs have additional income sources that can reduce their

Wealth Freedom Number. These might include rental properties, business royalties, intellectual property, or passive business investments. Calculate the reliable annual income from these sources and subtract it from your annual lifestyle cost before multiplying by 25.

For example, if rental properties generate $50,000 in reliable annual income and your lifestyle costs $200,000 each year, traditional investments would need to cover only $150,000. Your adjusted freedom number would be $3,750,000 ($150,000 × 25) rather than $5,000,000.

Adding large future expenses that your regular withdrawals cannot cover is the final step. These might include children's college costs, wedding expenses, major health care needs, parent support, or significant purchases. Add these future expenses to your Wealth Freedom Number to create your complete freedom target.

Your Wealth Freedom Number isn't static. Recalculate it annually as your lifestyle evolves and financial markets change. The safe withdrawal rate might need adjustment based on your investment approach and economic conditions. Some financial planners now recommend using a rate of 3% to 3.5% instead of 4% for more conservative planning that will increase the amount of capital you need.

Many entrepreneurs are shocked when they first calculate their Wealth Freedom Number. They've been building wealth without a target, often dramatically underestimating what they need. One business owner thought $2 million would make him financially free, but after proper calculation, he discovered that his freedom number was $6.8 million. This awareness completely transformed his business exit strategy and Wealth Timeline.

The power of knowing your precise Wealth Freedom Number cannot be overstated. It transforms wealth-building from a vague aspiration to a specific, measurable goal. It helps you evaluate business opportunities based on how they advance your freedom timeline. Most importantly, it gives you a clear finish line that tells you exactly when work becomes optional rather than financially necessary.

The Three Phases of Entrepreneurial Wealth

Every entrepreneur moves through three distinct phases on the journey from startup to financial freedom. Each phase requires entirely different wealth strategies, yet most business owners apply the same approaches regardless of where they stand. Understanding these three phases—Survival, Stability, and Significance—will transform how you build wealth and dramatically accelerate your journey to financial independence.

The Survival Phase characterizes most entrepreneurs in their first few years of business. During this phase, your primary financial focus is generating enough business income to cover basic living expenses. Your business requires constant cash infusions rather than producing excess capital for wealth-building. Your personal finances often suffer as you pour everything into making your company viable.

The wealth strategy during Survival focuses almost entirely on cash flow management and personal financial defense. You should maintain minimal emergency reserves and avoid major new personal debt, protect against catastrophic risks through basic insurance, and make only token wealth-building moves, like small retirement contributions—more to establish the habit than to build significant assets.

During Survival, trying to implement aggressive wealth-building strategies usually backfires. Simply put, you lack consistent capital, and business needs often force you to liquidate premature investments at losses. Your primary wealth goal in this phase should be surviving long enough to reach Stability while preventing major financial setbacks that could take years to recover from.

One entrepreneur in the Survival Phase tried implementing wealth strategies she read about in financial magazines. She invested aggressively in the stock market, purchased investment real estate with high leverage, and contributed heavily to retirement accounts. When her business faced a cash crunch, she was forced to liquidate investments at losses and tap retirement funds with penalties. She eventually lost the rental property to foreclosure. The right strategy would have been building business stability first, then wealth assets later.

The Stability Phase begins when your business consistently generates enough profit to cover your lifestyle with some excess capital remaining. Your company no longer requires constant personal cash infusions. You can pay yourself regularly and begin thinking beyond month-to-month finances. Most established entrepreneurs operate in this phase for many years before reaching Significance.

The wealth strategy during Stability focuses on systematic transfers from business to personal assets. You should implement the Wealth Transfer Protocol from Chapter 3, establish tax optimization strategies from Chapter 4, and begin building your Personal Wealth Engine from Chapter 5. Your primary focus shifts from nurturing business survival to creating parallel tracks of wealth growth—continuing to build your company while simultaneously developing assets outside the business.

During Stability, your wealth acceleration comes from increasing the percentage of business profit that transfers to personal assets rather than lifestyle expansion. The entrepreneurs who progress most quickly through this phase do so by maintaining flat personal spending even as business income grows, directing all additional capital to wealth-building vehicles. This creates compounding momentum that eventually leads to Significance.

A marketing agency owner entered the Stability Phase when her business reached $1.2 million in revenue with consistent profits. She implemented a systematic wealth transfer system that automatically moved 35% of all business profits to investment accounts before she could spend it on lifestyle. While friends with similar businesses upgraded to luxury cars and larger homes as their income grew, she maintained moderate spending and focused on building her Freedom Fund. Within seven years, her investments outside the business grew to over $1.8 million, while her peers had little to show for their higher incomes.

The Significance Phase begins when your assets outside the business generate enough passive income to cover a substantial portion of your lifestyle expenses—typically 30% to 50%. At this point, you've built significant wealth independent of your company, creating partial financial freedom. Work becomes increasingly optional rather than financially necessary.

The wealth strategy during Significance focuses on optimization and acceleration rather than foundation building. You should implement advanced tax strategies, explore alternative investments with higher returns, optimize asset location across account types, and begin transition planning for your business. Your primary focus shifts from building basic wealth to maximizing returns, minimizing taxes, and creating your ideal post-business life.

During Significance, wealth acceleration comes from leveraging what you've already built rather than working harder or taking greater risks. The entrepreneurs who progress most quickly through this final phase focus on maximizing business profit, increasing returns on existing assets, minimizing tax drag across their entire financial ecosystem, and strategically deploying their expertise in high-value opportunities that require capital but minimal time.

A technology company owner entered the Significance Phase with $2.7 million in investments that generated about 40% of his family's lifestyle expenses. Instead of continuing his previous wealth strategies, he implemented more sophisticated approaches: shifting from mutual funds to directly managed investments that increased his after-tax returns by 2.3% annually, restructuring his business entity to create additional tax advantages, and making strategic investments in other businesses where his expertise created outsized returns. These optimizations cut five years off his timeline to complete financial independence.

Understanding which phase you're in transforms your wealth-building effectiveness by ensuring that you implement the right strategies at the right time. Most entrepreneurs waste years applying Significance strategies during Survival or limiting themselves to Survival approaches during Stability. This phase mismatch creates frustration and dramatically slows wealth accumulation.

Each phase builds upon the previous one, creating a natural progression toward financial freedom. The Survival Phase establishes the business foundation that accelerates and produces excess capital. The Stability Phase creates the wealth transfer systems that build assets outside your company. The Significance Phase optimizes these assets to eventually replace your business income entirely.

The most important wealth decision you'll make this year is correctly identifying your current phase and implementing the appropriate strategies for where you stand. This single insight often eliminates years of misplaced effort and dramatically accelerates progress toward your freedom number.

Creating Your Wealth Timeline

Most entrepreneurs have no clear timeline for achieving financial freedom. They save and invest without knowing whether their current pace will create independence in five years, fifteen years, or never. This uncertainty leads to poor decisions, wasted opportunities, and unnecessary stress. Creating your Wealth Timeline—a realistic road map from your current position to complete wealth independence—solves this problem by showing exactly where you stand and what adjustments will accelerate your journey.

Your Wealth Timeline starts with three critical numbers: your current investable assets outside your business, your Wealth Freedom Number from the first section, and your current annual wealth-building (how much you're transferring from business to investments each year). These three figures form the foundation of your timeline calculation.

For example, let's say you currently have $500,000 in investments, your Wealth Freedom Number is $4 million, and you're building wealth at $100,000 annually. You can use these numbers to calculate a basic timeline. Assuming 7% average investment returns, you would reach your Wealth Freedom Number in approximately nineteen years. This baseline projection creates your starting point for timeline optimization.

Most entrepreneurs are shocked when they first calculate this basic timeline. They discover that their current pace will create freedom much later than expected—often well into their sixties or seventies, despite having successful businesses. One business owner was dismayed to learn his current $75,000 annual wealth-building would take twenty-six years to reach his $5.2 million freedom number, making him seventy-three before achieving financial independence.

The power of your Wealth Timeline comes from seeing exactly how changes to three key variables—wealth-building rate, investment returns, and Wealth Freedom Number—affect your years to independence. Small adjustments to these variables can dramatically accelerate your timeline, often cutting five to ten years from your journey without requiring massive business growth or lifestyle sacrifices.

The first timeline accelerator is increasing your wealth-building rate—the amount transferred annually from business to investments. This provides the most direct impact on your timeline. For example, increasing annual wealth-building from $100,000 to $150,000 would reduce the timeline from nineteen years to approximately fourteen—a five-year acceleration from this single change.

Wealth-building increases come from three primary sources: business profit growth, higher wealth transfer percentages, and reduced lifestyle costs. Most entrepreneurs focus exclusively on the first source while ignoring the other two, which often provide faster results with less effort. Increasing your wealth transfer percentage from 25% to 40% of business profit can accelerate your timeline more quickly than years of trying to grow revenue.

A service business owner was generating wealth at a rate of $120,000 per year, with a timeline of twenty-two years to reach her Wealth Freedom Number. Rather than focusing solely on growing her already-successful business, she implemented the Wealth Transfer Protocol from Chapter

3, increasing her transfer percentage from 20% to 35% of profits. This single change increased her annual wealth-building to $210,000, reducing her timeline to fourteen years without requiring any business growth.

The second timeline accelerator is improving your investment returns through better asset allocation, tax efficiency, and investment selection. While you can't control markets, you can significantly increase your after-tax returns by properly implementing the strategies in Chapter 5. Each 1% improvement in average annual returns typically reduces your timeline by two to three years.

For example, improving average returns from 7% to 9% in our initial example would reduce the timeline from nineteen years to approximately fifteen. Combined with the increased wealth-building rate from the previous example, the timeline would shrink to just twelve years—cutting seven years from the original projection through these two optimizations.

A technology entrepreneur discovered that his current investment approach was generating after-tax returns averaging just 5.2% annually, despite strong market performance. By implementing the tax integration strategies from Chapter 4 and the investment framework from Chapter 5, he increased his after-tax returns to 7.8% without taking additional risk. This 2.6% improvement reduced his timeline by nearly six years.

The third timeline accelerator is refining your Wealth Freedom Number by optimizing your lifestyle and adding income sources. This doesn't mean sacrificing quality of life, but rather identifying which expenses create happiness and which simply inflate your required capital. Each $10,000 reduction in annual lifestyle cost reduces your Wealth Freedom Number by $250,000, potentially cutting years from your timeline.

Additionally, developing passive income sources—like rental properties, business royalties, or intellectual property—can significantly reduce the investment assets you need for independence. Each $20,000 in reliable annual passive income reduces your Wealth Freedom Number by $500,000, substantially accelerating your timeline.

One business owner reduced his Wealth Freedom Number from $6.2 million to $4.8 million through two strategic moves: eliminating $30,000 in annual expenses that didn't meaningfully contribute to his happiness and developing a rental property portfolio generating $40,000 in reliable annual income. These changes cut his timeline by eight years without requiring him to reduce his quality of life.

Your complete Wealth Timeline should include quarterly milestones that create accountability and allow regular progress measurement. These milestones break your journey into manageable segments with targets for investable assets, wealth-building rate, and investment returns at each checkpoint. This detailed road map transforms a distant goal into a series of achievable steps with clear metrics for success.

For example, rather than simply targeting $4 million in fifteen years, your timeline might specify reaching $750,000 within three years, $1.6 million within seven years, and $2.8 million within eleven years, with wealth-building targets for each period. These interim milestones create momentum and allow course correction if you fall behind pace.

A manufacturing business owner created a detailed timeline with quarterly milestones toward his $3.8 million Wealth Freedom Number. When he fell behind after the first year, the clear metrics prompted immediate adjustments to his wealth transfer system rather than allowing the gap to widen. This accountability accelerated his wealth-building from $90,000 to $140,000 annually, putting him back on track toward his twelve-year independence goal.

Your Wealth Timeline becomes the strategic foundation for business and investment decisions. Rather than evaluating opportunities in isolation, you can assess them based on how they affect your years to freedom. This clarity often leads to counterintuitive choices that prioritize an accelerated timeline over traditional business or investment metrics.

For example, one entrepreneur might choose to maintain a smaller, highly profitable business with lower stress and higher wealth transfer potential rather than pursuing aggressive growth that demands constant reinvestment. Another might select slightly lower-return investments with more reliable outcomes to ensure timeline predictability. These strategic choices emerge naturally when you have a clear freedom road map guiding your decisions.

Protecting Your Wealth Journey

Building wealth means nothing if you can't protect it. Most entrepreneurs focus entirely on accumulation while ignoring the critical protection strategies that keep market downturns, business challenges, or personal crises from derailing their wealth journey. Without proper protection, years of wealth-building can evaporate in months—or even days—setting your freedom timeline back a decade or more.

Wealth protection isn't about fear or pessimism. It's about making sure that the inevitable challenges every entrepreneur faces don't permanently damage your progress toward financial independence. Effective protection strategies foster resilience, enabling your wealth to withstand challenges instead of succumbing to them.

The first essential protection is business continuity coverage. Your business generates the capital that powers your entire wealth journey, making its continued operation your most important financial asset. Yet most entrepreneurs lack comprehensive protection against the events most likely to interrupt their business income.

Effective business continuity coverage includes key person insurance that protects against the financial consequences of death or disability of essential team members (including yourself), proper liability coverage for your industry risks, and cyber protection against increasingly common digital threats.

One technology company owner had built substantial personal wealth but left his business vulnerable through inadequate continuity coverage. When a key developer suffered a serious health crisis and couldn't work for six months, the business faced significant delivery delays and client losses. Without proper key person coverage, the owner was forced to liquidate over $300,000 in personal investments to keep the company afloat—setting his Wealth Timeline back nearly three years.

The second essential protection is market volatility buffering. Every wealth journey encounters multiple market downturns, with typical corrections of 20% to 30% occurring every five to seven years and major crashes of 40% to 50% happening every ten to fifteen years. Without proper buffering strategies, these inevitable declines can devastate your timeline, especially if they occur near your target freedom date.

Effective volatility buffering includes maintaining appropriate cash reserves (typically one to two years of planned withdrawals as you approach your freedom date), implementing strategic asset allocation that matches your timeline horizon, using tactical hedging during periods of extreme valuation, and, most importantly, having predetermined response plans for different market scenarios.

A service business owner was just two years from her freedom target when the 2008 financial crisis hit, reducing her portfolio by over 40%. Without proper volatility buffering, she was forced to delay her exit for seven additional years while rebuilding her assets. Had she implemented appropriate buffering strategies as she approached her target, the same market event would have delayed her timeline by only one to two years.

The third essential protection is tax risk management. Tax laws change constantly, and strategies that work today may be eliminated tomorrow. Entrepreneurs who concentrate their wealth in single tax strategies often face devastating setbacks when legislation changes, forcing dramatic timeline revisions.

Effective tax risk management includes diversifying across tax treatment types (pre-tax, post-tax, and tax-advantaged accounts), maintaining flexibility to adapt to changing laws, implementing strategies with established legal precedent rather than aggressive positions, and working with advisors who focus on sustainable approaches rather than exploiting temporary loopholes.

The fourth essential protection is lifestyle lockdown as you approach your freedom target. Many entrepreneurs undermine their wealth journey by expanding their lifestyles just as they are about to reach their goal. Each significant lifestyle increase requires additional capital to sustain, potentially adding years to your timeline at the very point when freedom was within reach.

An effective lifestyle lockdown includes making major standard-of-living decisions early in your wealth journey rather than continuously upgrading, separating true happiness-producing expenses from status-driven costs, creating clear boundaries around lifestyle inflation as your wealth grows, and focusing on experiences rather than possessions that require ongoing maintenance.

A technology entrepreneur was within eighteen months of his freedom target when he decided to purchase a vacation home requiring $60,000 in additional annual expenses. This single decision increased his Wealth Freedom Number by $1.5 million, adding over four years to his timeline despite being nearly complete. Had he deferred this purchase until after achieving his original freedom goal, he could have made a more informed choice from a position of financial independence rather than extending his mandatory work period.

The fifth essential protection is family financial alignment. Many wealth journeys derail not through business or market issues but through family financial conflicts. Spouses with different money values, children with unsustainable expectations, or extended family emergencies often create the largest wealth disruptions yet receive the least planning.

Effective family alignment includes creating clear wealth values and communications with spouses and partners, developing appropriate financial education for children that manages expectations, establishing boundaries around family financial assistance, and implementing proper estate planning that protects assets across generations.

I worked with a business owner a few years ago who had built substantial wealth but never discussed financial values or expectations with his spouse, who had very different perspectives on spending and risk. When market volatility temporarily reduced their portfolio value, these unaddressed differences created significant conflict. The resulting divorce settlement divided their assets and dramatically increased expenses, adding over a decade to his freedom timeline. Regular financial alignment conversations would have identified and addressed these differences before they threatened their wealth journey.

The sixth essential protection is precision insurance coverage. Most entrepreneurs are either dramatically underinsured against catastrophic risks or overinsured against manageable ones. Both extremes damage your

Wealth Timeline—the first through devastating setbacks from unprotected events, and the second through excessive premiums that reduce wealth-building capacity.

Effective insurance precision includes maintaining high-limit, high-deductible coverage for catastrophic risks (liability, serious disability, major health events) while self-insuring smaller risks that won't materially damage your wealth journey. This balanced approach provides protection where needed while maximizing capital available for wealth-building.

A professional services firm owner I coached was spending over $40,000 annually on insurance premiums for numerous overlapping policies with low deductibles. After implementing precision coverage—increasing deductibles, eliminating redundant policies, and adding a single high-limit umbrella policy—she reduced her annual premiums to $15,000 while improving protection against major risks. The $25,000 annual savings accelerated her wealth-building, reducing her timeline by nearly two years while maintaining appropriate protection.

These six protection essentials work together to create a resilient wealth journey that can withstand the inevitable challenges every entrepreneur faces. Without them, your path to financial independence remains vulnerable to disruptions that can erase years of progress in moments of crisis.

The most effective approach implements protection strategies in phases aligned with your wealth journey. During the Survival Phase, focus on catastrophic risk protection and basic business continuity. During the Stability Phase, add market volatility buffering and tax risk management. During the Significance Phase, implement lifestyle lockdown and sophisticated family alignment strategies.

This phased implementation protects you against the most relevant risks at each stage without overwhelming your finances with premature strategies. The goal isn't to eliminate all risk, which is impossible. Instead, it's to ensure that no single event can permanently derail your progress toward financial independence.

Chapter 7 Recap: Mapping Your Path to Wealth Independence

You now have the complete blueprint for transforming business success into personal financial freedom. Throughout this chapter, we've mapped the journey from your current position to complete wealth independence, creating a clear path that eliminates guesswork and accelerates your timeline.

Key Insights

Wealth Freedom Number

- The precise amount of wealth required outside your business to maintain your lifestyle without working.
- Calculated by:
    1. Assessing true current expenses.
    2. Adjusting for future changes (e.g., inflation, lifestyle shifts).
    3. Incorporating additional income sources.
    4. Adding major future costs (e.g., education, healthcare).
- This target turns wealth-building into a measurable, actionable goal.

The Three Phases of Entrepreneurial Wealth

- **Survival**: Focus on reducing financial vulnerability and stabilizing income.
- **Stability**: Build consistent wealth outside your business.
- **Significance**: Shift to legacy planning and maximizing long-term impact.

Each phase requires unique strategies tailored to your current financial situation and goals.

The Wealth Timeline

- A roadmap showing how long it will take to reach financial independence at your current pace.
- Adjusting three variables can dramatically accelerate your timeline:
  1. **Wealth-Building Rate**: Increase money transferred to personal assets.
  2. **Investment Returns**: Optimize portfolio performance.
  3. **Wealth Freedom Number**: Adjust lifestyle expectations or additional income sources.
- Small, strategic changes can cut 5-10 years off your timeline.

Six Protection Essentials

- Safeguards to prevent setbacks during your wealth journey:
  1. **Business Continuity Coverage**: Protect against operational disruptions.
  2. **Market Volatility Buffering**: Reduce portfolio risk with diversification and cash reserves.
  3. **Tax Risk Management**: Minimize tax liabilities over time.
  4. **Lifestyle Lockdown**: Prevent lifestyle inflation from derailing wealth-building.
  5. **Family Financial Alignment**: Ensure shared financial goals and practices.
  6. **Precision Insurance Coverage**: Protect assets with tailored insurance policies.

Action Steps

1. Calculate Your Wealth Freedom Number

- Use your current expenses, future adjustments, and additional income sources to determine your target.
- This becomes the foundation for all wealth-building efforts.

2. Identify Your Current Wealth Phase

- Determine whether you're in **Survival**, **Stability**, or **Significance**.
- Focus on strategies specific to your phase to maximize efficiency and avoid premature tactics.

3. Create Your Wealth Timeline

- Map out quarterly milestones for the next five years:
  - Targets for investable assets.
  - Wealth-building rate increases.
  - Key protection strategies to implement.
- Use this timeline to stay accountable and measure progress.

4. Implement Protection Strategies

- Start with essential safeguards for your current phase, such as:
  - Business continuity coverage for Survival Phase.
  - Market buffering for Stability Phase.

        - Legacy planning for Significance Phase.
    - Add additional protections as your wealth grows.

Key Takeaways for Transformation

- **Clarity and Confidence**: Know exactly where you stand on your journey to financial independence.
- **Accelerated Progress**: Strategically optimize resources to cut years off your timeline without working harder.
- **Resilience**: Protect your wealth journey against inevitable business, market, and personal challenges.

Next Steps in the Book

- Learn advanced methods for scaling wealth-building efforts during the Significance Phase.
- Explore techniques for simplifying wealth management as your net worth grows.
- Discover strategies for aligning purpose and legacy with financial independence.

By following this plan, you'll transform financial freedom from an abstract idea into a concrete, achievable goal. Your entrepreneurial success will translate into lasting wealth, giving you the freedom to choose your future based on purpose rather than necessity.

Chapter 8

The Wealthy Entrepreneur Lifestyle

The Psychology of Wealth

Most entrepreneurs get stuck thinking about money in the wrong way. They work hard in their business and make good money, but they still feel anxious about their finances. This happens because making money and building wealth require entirely different mindsets. You can be great at earning income through your business but terrible at building lasting wealth. The income game and the wealth game are two different games, and you must win at both of them as a business owner and entrepreneur.

The wealth mindset starts with separating your identity from your business. Many entrepreneurs define their worth by their company's performance. When business is good, they feel rich. When business slows down, they feel poor—even if they have substantial assets. This emotional roller coaster prevents consistent wealth-building because it leads to reactive financial decisions based on temporary business conditions.

I worked with a client who built a $3 million HVAC company. On paper, he looked successful. But his self-worth rose and fell with each month's revenue. During good months, he spent freely and felt confident. During slower months, he froze all personal wealth transfers and lived in fear. This pattern kept him on a money treadmill, even though he'd earned high six figures for years. His business made money, but he never built wealth because his psychology wouldn't allow consistent wealth-building habits.

The wealth mindset requires you to see yourself as separate from your business. Your company becomes an asset you own—not your identity. This separation allows you to make rational wealth decisions regardless of normal business fluctuations. You continue building personal assets, even during business challenges, because you understand that consistent wealth transfers matter more than timing the perfect moment.

Another critical shift happens when you start valuing assets over income. Most entrepreneurs focus entirely on increasing business revenue and profit. And that is understandable and necessary for survival. They get excited about making more money but pay little attention to owning more assets. This focus on income creates what we call a "treadmill entrepreneur"; it's like a hamster wheel. You work harder each year, but you never feel financially secure because income requires constant effort. Assets, meanwhile, work for you.

Wealth-minded entrepreneurs track their personal asset growth as carefully as they track their business income growth. They get more excited about adding $100,000 to their investment portfolio than adding $100,000 to their business revenue. They understand that income feeds today's lifestyle, while assets create tomorrow's freedom. This simple shift in focus dramatically changes financial behaviors and results.

One business owner I advised had been earning over $500,000 annually for eight years but had accumulated less than $200,000 in assets outside her business. After shifting her focus to asset growth, she began tracking her net worth quarterly and celebrating asset milestones. Within three years, her outside investments had grown to over $700,000, while her income remained roughly the same. The difference wasn't in earning more—it was in paying attention to different metrics.

The third psychological shift involves embracing delayed gratification. Most entrepreneurs have a strong drive to achieve that creates success in business, but that same drive often undermines wealth-building. They want results now. This impatience works for business growth, where hustle creates faster outcomes. But wealth-building rewards patience and consistency over intensity. The entrepreneurs who build significant wealth aren't necessarily those who earn the most. They are the ones who consistently save and invest over time.

This patience extends to investment approaches. Wealth-minded entrepreneurs resist chasing hot investments or making frequent changes to their portfolio. They understand that wealth comes from allowing compound growth to work over decades, not from finding the next big thing or timing market movements. This patient approach feels boring compared to the excitement of business growth but creates far better long-term results.

A professional services firm owner had changed investment approaches six times in five years, constantly chasing better returns. Each change created transaction costs, tax consequences, and disrupted compound growth. After adopting a patient wealth psychology, she selected a sound investment strategy and committed to maintaining it with only minor adjustments for at least ten years. This consistency increased her returns by over 3% annually compared to her previous approach. Warren Buffett famously said, "Money is like a bar of soap; the more you handle it, the less you have."

The fourth psychological shift involves developing an appropriate risk perspective. Most entrepreneurs take substantial risks in their businesses but then either become too conservative or too aggressive with their investments. Neither extreme serves wealth-building. The wealth mindset balances risk across your entire financial life rather than viewing business and personal finances separately.

Since entrepreneurs already take significant risk with their primary income source, their investment approach should provide balance rather than amplifying business risk. This often means taking a different approach with investments than traditional advisors might recommend for someone your age. The goal isn't to maximize returns in isolation but to optimize your entire financial picture for both growth and security.

One technology entrepreneur had 80% of his investments in tech stocks similar to his own business. When the tech sector experienced a downturn, both his business and personal investments suffered simultaneously. After developing a proper risk perspective, he restructured his portfolio to include more stable assets that would likely perform well when his business faced challenges. This balance created true financial security rather than just potential for higher returns.

The fifth psychological shift involves developing a mindset of abundance. Many entrepreneurs operate from scarcity mindsets despite their success. They worry about losing money, focus on cutting out things in their lives that bring them joy rather than growing wealth, and make decisions from fear rather than opportunity. This scarcity thinking creates tight-fisted approaches that reduce wealth-building potential.

Wealth-minded entrepreneurs develop abundance thinking that focuses on growth, opportunity, and possibility. They make financial decisions based on potential returns rather than potential losses. They invest in quality advice rather than seeking the cheapest options. Instead of avoiding all tax expenses, they concentrate on optimizing their tax strategy. This abundance approach feels counterintuitive but creates substantially better results.

A business owner who had always prepared his own taxes and run his own QuickBooks to save money finally invested in a specialized tax strategist. The professional fee was $3,000 per month—far more than the $800 tax software he previously used. But the strategist identified legitimate tax strategies that saved over $42,000 in the first year alone. The abundance mindset of investing in quality advice rather than minimizing all costs created immediate positive returns.

Developing wealth psychology doesn't happen overnight. It requires conscious effort to reshape thought patterns established over years or decades. The most effective approach combines daily mindset practices with environmental changes that support new thinking patterns.

Time Wealth: The Ultimate Currency

Money matters. But time matters more. You can always make more money, but you can never make more time. Creating time wealth, or the freedom to spend your limited hours on this planet doing what matters most to you, is the true purpose of building financial wealth. We call it TruWealth, and that's why we gave our firm that name. Yet many entrepreneurs get so caught up in chasing financial wealth that they never achieve the time wealth that was their original goal.

Time wealth means controlling your calendar. It means waking up each day and choosing how to spend your hours based on purpose and joy rather than financial necessity. It means working because you want to, not because you have to. This freedom and flexibility represent the ultimate form of wealth, yet it remains elusive for most successful entrepreneurs who find themselves working harder each year despite growing financial success.

The journey to time wealth starts with a critical mindset shift—seeing time as your most valuable nonrenewable resource. Most entrepreneurs unconsciously value money above time. They'll spend hours saving a few thousand dollars but won't invest money to buy back their time. They'll work all weekend to avoid hiring help. They'll handle low-value tasks themselves rather than delegating. These choices might save money, but they squander something far more precious.

Wealth-mindedentrepreneurs—TruWealthentrepreneurs—flip this equation. They ruthlessly evaluate how they spend their time and search for opportunities to buy back hours through strategic spending. They ask, "What's the highest and best use of my time?" and eliminate, automate, or delegate everything else. This approach often requires spending more money in the short term but creates both time and financial wealth in the long run.

One business owner tracked her time for two weeks and discovered she spent over fifteen hours weekly on administrative tasks she could delegate for $25 per hour. By hiring help, she invested $375 weekly to reclaim fifteen hours. She used those hours to focus on business development activities that generated over $2,000 in new weekly revenue. This strategy increased her financial wealth while giving her more control over her calendar.

The principle of time wealth involves creating clear boundaries between wealth-building work and wealth-enjoying time. Most entrepreneurs let work expand to fill all available hours. They check emails at dinner, take calls on weekends, and never fully disconnect. This constant connection creates the illusion of productivity but reduces effectiveness while preventing the rejuvenation that comes from true time wealth.

Effective time wealth strategies include creating technology boundaries (no work emails after seven p.m.), physical boundaries (a separate workspace), and calendar boundaries (blocked personal time that's non-negotiable). These boundaries don't reduce productivity—they enhance it by keeping you fully present for both work and personal time rather than constantly distracted during either.

A marketing agency owner implemented strict boundaries by turning off work notifications on his phone from six p.m. to eight a.m. and keeping weekends completely work-free. His team adapted by handling more decisions independently, and clients respected the clear expectations. Contrary to his fears, business didn't suffer. In fact, it improved because he returned to work more focused and creative after genuine breaks. His income remained the same while his life satisfaction dramatically increased.

The third principle involves strategically using financial wealth to create time wealth through leverage. Many entrepreneurs build significant financial assets but never convert them into time freedom. They continue working the same hours despite having more than enough money to scale back. Habits, an attachment to one's work identity, and a fear of change are behind this failure to convert financial wealth into time wealth.

Effective strategies include hiring executive support (not just administrative help but high-level professionals who can replace your thinking and decision-making), creating passive income streams that require minimal oversight, and strategically reducing business responsibilities by delegating or restructuring. These approaches convert financial capital into time capital.

One professional services firm owner had built substantial investments but still worked sixty-plus hours a week. After implementing leverage strategies, she hired a senior professional who could handle 70% of her client load, restructured her business to focus only on ideal clients, and created systems that eliminated her operational responsibilities. These changes reduced her work hours to twenty-five per week while maintaining 85% of her income. Her financial wealth ultimately allowed her to gain more free time.

The fourth principle involves creating your ideal week design. Most entrepreneurs react to demands rather than intentionally structuring their time. They let clients, team members, and emergencies dictate their calendar rather than allocating time based on their priorities. This reactive approach hinders them from achieving true time wealth, even when they're financially successful.

Creating your ideal week means designing exactly how you'd spend your time if you had complete control, then gradually shifting your schedule toward this ideal. This design includes specific times for deep work, team interaction, personal rejuvenation, family connection, and health activities. It becomes the template against which you evaluate all time requests.

A technology company owner created his ideal week with mornings reserved for creative work, afternoons for team and client interaction, and Fridays completely free for learning and reflection. He then restructured his business operations to support this design, including changing meeting schedules, client expectations, and team responsibilities. Within six months, his calendar matched his ideal design 80% of the time, creating substantial time wealth while improving business performance.

The fifth principle involves implementing strategic incompetence in areas that don't leverage your unique abilities. Many entrepreneurs pride themselves on being capable in many domains. This jack-of-all-trades approach creates time poverty by pulling you into tasks others could handle better. Wealth-minded entrepreneurs deliberately remain strategically incompetent in areas outside their genius zone, forcing them to delegate rather than get involved.

Strategic incompetence might mean never learning certain software systems, avoiding specific operational areas, or deliberately not developing skills that others have. This selective focus creates time wealth by keeping you engaged only in activities where your contribution creates exceptional value.

A consulting firm owner realized he spent hours every week formatting client presentations, despite having team members who could do it better. He deliberately remained incompetent at the newest presentation software, making it impossible for this task to fall back on his plate. This strategic incompetence freed several hours a week while improving the final product through specialized talent.

The journey to time wealth requires the same intentional approach as financial wealth-building. It doesn't happen automatically when you reach a certain income or net worth. Many financially wealthy entrepreneurs remain time poor because they never implement the strategies that convert money into freedom. TruWealth includes both financial security and time abundance—the ultimate currency that makes all other successes meaningful.

From Success to Significance

Making money feels good. Building wealth feels better. But creating meaning through your wealth feels best. Most entrepreneurs focus entirely on success—growing their business, increasing their income, and building their net worth. But at some point, usually in their forties or fifties, they start asking deeper questions:

- "Is this all there is?"
- "What's the point of all this money?"
- "How can my wealth create something meaningful beyond just more wealth?"

These questions mark the critical transition from success to significance.

The significance journey starts with clarifying your wealth purpose. Most entrepreneurs never ask why they're building wealth beyond vague notions of security or freedom. Without a clear purpose, wealth accumulation becomes an endless treadmill with no meaningful destination. Defining a purpose for your wealth creates both motivation during the building phase and fulfillment when you begin deploying assets for impact.

Your wealth purpose might include creating family security across generations, funding causes you care deeply about, solving problems in your community, or creating opportunities for others who lack resources. The purpose matters less than the clarity that guides both wealth-building and wealth-deployment decisions.

One business owner realized that his core wealth purpose was creating educational opportunities for first-generation college students like himself. This clarity transformed his relationship with money. Building wealth became more meaningful because each dollar moved him closer to significant impact. His investment decisions, business strategy, and spending choices all aligned around this central purpose, creating both greater wealth and deeper fulfillment.

The second principle involves creating your legacy design. Most entrepreneurs think about legacy only in terms of what happens after they're gone. But significance-minded entrepreneurs design legacy systems that create impact during their lifetime while establishing frameworks for continued influence beyond their years. This living-legacy approach creates immediate meaning while building toward long-term significance.

Effective legacy design includes three components: values transmission (how your core values continue influencing others), wealth deployment (how your assets create impact aligned with your purpose), and knowledge transfer (how your wisdom and experience benefit future generations). These components work together to create significance that transcends financial success.

A technology entrepreneur created her legacy design in her early fifties rather than waiting for retirement or estate planning. She established a family foundation that involved her children in philanthropic decisions, created a structured mentoring program for emerging entrepreneurs in her field, and documented her business wisdom through recorded conversations and written materials. These activities created immediate significance while establishing frameworks for continued impact.

To maximize the impact of your resources, the third principle calls for strategic giving. Many successful entrepreneurs engage in reactive charitable giving—writing checks to whoever asks or supporting random causes without a clear strategy. This scattered approach creates minimal impact despite generous intentions. Significance-minded entrepreneurs implement strategic giving approaches that align their resources with their deepest values and create measurable outcomes.

Strategic giving includes focusing on impact areas rather than spreading resources too thinly, conducting due diligence on organizations similar to business investment analysis, establishing clear metrics for evaluating results, and leveraging not just financial capital but also your expertise, network, and influence. This focused approach creates a substantially greater impact from the same resources.

A manufacturing business owner had been giving to dozens of different causes but felt a minimal connection to the outcomes. After implementing strategic giving, he focused 80% of his philanthropic resources on developing the workforce in his community—an area where he had deep knowledge and networks. By combining financial support with his expertise and business connections, he helped create a training program that moved hundreds of people into living-wage jobs while addressing his industry's talent shortage. This focused approach created a meaningful impact that random giving never achieved.

The fourth principle involves wealth stewardship rather than just wealth ownership. Most entrepreneurs see their assets as personal property they can use however they wish. Significance-minded entrepreneurs develop stewardship thinking—seeing themselves as temporary managers of resources that can serve purposes beyond personal benefit. This mindset shift creates greater responsibility and meaning without diminishing how you enjoy your hard-earned wealth.

Stewardship thinking asks different questions about wealth decisions:

- "How can these resources serve multiple purposes beyond just my enjoyment?"
- "What's the highest use of this capital for both personal and broader benefit?"
- "How can I enjoy prosperity while creating opportunity for others?"

These questions lead to wealth deployment that creates both personal satisfaction and meaningful impact.

The fifth principle involves creating your wisdom transfer system. Most entrepreneurs accumulate invaluable knowledge through years of business experience, but this wisdom often dies with them or benefits only a few direct contacts. Significance-minded entrepreneurs develop systematic approaches for sharing their hard-earned insights with future generations, extending their impact far beyond their immediate circle or lifetime.

Effective wisdom transfer includes documenting your guiding principles and key learnings, creating mentoring structures that accommodate your available time, participating in knowledge-sharing platforms relevant to your expertise, and potentially creating educational content that scales your influence. These approaches leverage your intellectual capital for significance just as you leverage your financial capital.

The journey from success to significance doesn't require abandoning business achievement or wealth-building. It means adding deeper layers of meaning and purpose to financial success. The entrepreneurs who make this transition often discover that significance accelerates success as their clear purpose creates greater motivation, attracts aligned opportunities, and establishes meaningful differentiation in the marketplace. The integration of success and significance creates both prosperity and purpose—the true measure of a wealthy entrepreneur's achievement.

The Daily Practices of Wealthy Entrepreneurs

Wealth doesn't happen by accident. It happens through daily habits that seem small in the moment but compound dramatically over time. The entrepreneurs who build lasting wealth don't just have better strategies—they have better daily practices. These routines might take just minutes each day, but they create the consistent actions and decisions that ultimately determine your financial future.

The first essential practice is the morning money mindset routine. Most entrepreneurs start their day reacting to emails, messages, and urgent business matters. This reactive beginning creates a day of responding to others' priorities rather than advancing your wealth objectives. Wealthy entrepreneurs instead begin with a brief but powerful routine that sets their financial focus before the day's chaos begins.

An effective morning money routine takes just five to ten minutes but includes four key elements:

- Reviewing your current wealth metrics (net worth, investment performance, Wealth Ratio)
- Visualizing your wealth goals as already achieved
- Reading or listening to wealth-building content that reinforces productive financial thinking
- Setting your top wealth-building priority for the day

This simple routine creates both awareness and intention that shape financial decisions throughout your day.

One business owner implemented a seven-minute morning wealth routine. She reviewed her net worth tracker, read one page from a financial book, visualized her Wealth Freedom Number as achieved, and identified one wealth-building action for the day. This simple practice, maintained consistently for eighteen months, completely transformed her financial behaviors. Her wealth transfer rate increased from 8% to 27% of business profits, her investment consistency improved dramatically, and her net worth grew 118% during this period despite only modest business growth.

The second essential practice is decision filtering through wealth impact analysis. Most entrepreneurs make dozens of financial decisions daily without considering their long-term wealth impact. They evaluate choices based on immediate business needs, current cash flow, or emotional factors rather than systematic analysis of wealth effects. Wealthy entrepreneurs filter decisions through a quick mental framework that considers long-term financial impact alongside other factors.

Effective decision filtering involves asking three questions before any significant financial choice:

- "How does this affect my wealth-building rate?"
- "Does this move me toward or away from my Wealth Freedom Number?"
- "Is there a way to achieve the same outcome with a better wealth impact?"

This simple mental filter takes seconds to apply but dramatically improves the quality of decisions over time.

A service business owner began filtering decisions through wealth impact analysis. When considering a business expansion that required significant capital, he evaluated not just the business growth potential but also how the investment would affect his personal Wealth Timeline. This analysis led him to structure the expansion differently—using strategic partnerships rather than direct investment. And he achieved similar business outcomes while maintaining his wealth-building momentum. This single filtered decision preserved over $200,000 for personal wealth-building that would otherwise have been tied up in business assets.

The third essential practice is the wealth transfer trigger system. Most entrepreneurs handle wealth transfers reactively, moving money from business to personal accounts when they happen to think about it or when excess cash accumulates. This inconsistent approach creates sporadic wealth-building that falls victim to business cycles and competing priorities. Wealthy entrepreneurs instead establish automatic triggers that initiate transfers based on specific conditions rather than conscious decisions.

Effective trigger systems include threshold transfers (automatically moving money when business accounts exceed certain balances), percentage transfers (automatically directing set percentages of all revenue or profit), calendar transfers (scheduled movements regardless of business conditions), and milestone transfers (special movements when business achievements occur). These triggers create wealth-building consistency that doesn't require constant attention or willpower.

The fourth essential practice is the forty-eight-hour pause before lifestyle expansions. Most entrepreneurs increase their spending whenever business improves, creating lifestyle inflation that prevents wealth accumulation despite growing income. This automatic spending expansion happens because purchases are made emotionally in the moment. Wealthy entrepreneurs instead implement a simple waiting period before any significant lifestyle expense, creating space for rational evaluation rather than emotional decision-making.

The forty-eight-hour pause works by simply delaying any nonessential purchase over a certain amount (typically $500 to $1,000) for at least two days. During this period, you evaluate the purchase against your wealth objectives, consider alternatives, and make a rational rather than emotional decision. This brief delay doesn't prevent you from enjoying your success but ensures that lifestyle expenses remain intentional rather than automatic.

A marketing agency owner implemented the forty-eight-hour pause for any purchase over $750. When considering a luxury car upgrade that would increase his monthly expenses by $1,100, the pause gave him time to evaluate the true value of this lifestyle expansion against his wealth goals. He ultimately chose a more modest upgrade that increased costs by only $300 monthly and directed the difference toward investments. Over five years, this single paused decision created over $60,000 in additional wealth through reduced expenses and investment growth.

The fifth essential practice is the weekly wealth review. Most entrepreneurs review business performance regularly but evaluate their personal finances only occasionally—perhaps monthly, quarterly, or even annually. This infrequent review creates a disconnection from wealth progress and allows small negative patterns to continue for too long before correction. Wealthy entrepreneurs instead conduct brief but regular reviews that maintain awareness and enable quick adjustments.

An effective weekly review takes just fifteen to twenty minutes but includes five key elements:

- Tracking wealth transfers from business to personal accounts
- Reviewing investment contributions and performance
- Identifying any upcoming wealth-building opportunities or threats
- Evaluating progress toward Wealth Freedom Number milestones
- Setting wealth priorities for the coming week

This simple routine creates both accountability and agility in your wealth journey.

A professional services firm owner implemented a fifteen-minute Sunday evening wealth review. This consistent practice helped him identify that several planned wealth transfers hadn't occurred due to a banking change, his investment contributions had fallen significantly behind schedule, and an upcoming tax deadline created an opportunity for additional retirement contributions. Addressing these issues immediately rather than discovering them months later preserved thousands in wealth-building momentum and tax advantages.

The sixth essential practice is continuous wealth education. Most entrepreneurs focus their learning entirely on business growth, marketing, leadership, or technical skills related to their industry. They rarely dedicate time to developing their wealth-building knowledge. Wealthy entrepreneurs instead commit to regular financial education that compounds over time just like their investments.

Effective wealth education doesn't require hours of study. It might include reading one financial article daily, listening to wealth-building podcasts during commutes, reading one money-focused book monthly, attending quarterly webinars on wealth topics, or participating in mastermind groups focused on personal finance alongside business growth. This consistent exposure to financial wisdom shapes decisions and strategies far more effectively than occasional intensive study.

A technology business owner dedicated just fifteen minutes daily to wealth education through articles, books, and podcasts. Over eighteen months, this modest commitment dramatically improved his financial knowledge and decision-making. He restructured his business entities to reduce taxes by over $70,000 annually, implemented investment approaches that increased his returns by approximately 3.2% while reducing risk, and established wealth protection strategies he previously didn't know existed. These improvements stemmed directly from consistent small doses of financial education rather than any single learning experience.

The power of these daily practices comes from their consistency rather than their intensity. A ten-minute morning routine maintained for years creates far more wealth impact than occasional financial planning sessions. A brief weekly review sustained for decades builds more wealth than sporadic intensive analysis. The wealthy entrepreneurs who maintain these simple practices build fortunes not through financial brilliance but through consistent application of fundamental principles that compound over time.

Chapter 8 Recap: Living as a Wealthy Entrepreneur

You now understand the essential elements of the wealthy entrepreneur lifestyle—the daily practices, psychological shifts, and strategic approaches that transform business success into true financial freedom and significance. Let's recap what you've learned and outline your immediate action steps to implement these principles in your life and business.

Key Insights

The Psychology of Wealth

- Mindset shifts that distinguish lasting wealth-builders from high earners:
  - Separate your identity from your business.
  - Value **assets** over income.
  - Embrace **delayed gratification** for long-term wealth.
  - Develop a balanced risk perspective.
  - Cultivate **abundance thinking** to unlock opportunities.

Time Wealth as the Ultimate Currency

- Financial wealth gains meaning when it buys back time.
- Key time-focused strategies:
  - Treat time as your most valuable resource.
  - Set **clear boundaries** to protect it.
  - Leverage wealth to **delegate, automate, or eliminate** low-value tasks.
  - Design your **ideal week** to reflect your purpose and joy.
  - Use **strategic incompetence** to intentionally avoid tasks that don't serve you.

From Success to Significance

- Transition wealth from personal benefit to lasting impact:
  - Clarify your **wealth purpose**—the deeper "why" of your financial goals.
  - Draft your **legacy design** to guide your wealth's long-term impact.
  - Embrace **strategic giving** to align philanthropy with your values.
  - Develop a **stewardship mindset**, viewing wealth as a tool for meaningful impact.
  - Establish **wisdom transfer systems** to extend your knowledge and values across generations.

Daily Practices of Wealthy Entrepreneurs

- Simple routines that create consistent wealth-building habits:
  - **Morning Money Mindset Routine**: Reflect on gratitude, goals, and purpose daily.
  - **Decision Filtering**: Use wealth impact analysis to evaluate decisions.
  - **Wealth Transfer Trigger System**: Automate transfers from business to personal assets.
  - **48-Hour Pause Rule**: Delay lifestyle expansions to prevent impulsive spending.
  - **Weekly Wealth Review**: Assess progress and address challenges regularly.
  - **Continuous Wealth Education**: Stay informed and adapt to new opportunities.

Action Steps

1. Implement the Morning Wealth Mindset Routine

- Select three elements from the routine that resonate with you (e.g., gratitude, visualization, or reviewing goals).
- Spend 5-7 minutes on this practice each morning before engaging with emails or work.

2. Create Your Time Buyback Plan

- Identify three activities consuming your time that can be:
  - Eliminated, automated, or delegated.
- Calculate the financial cost of reclaiming this time versus the potential return (e.g., higher-value activities or personal rejuvenation).
- Implement at least one strategy to reclaim time within the next week.

3. Draft Your Initial Legacy Statement

- Write 1-2 paragraphs describing the impact you want your wealth to create beyond yourself.
- Share this statement with a spouse or trusted advisor to foster accountability and refine your vision.

4. Select Three Daily Practices to Implement

- Choose the three routines that align most closely with your priorities (e.g., weekly wealth review, decision filtering, or 48-hour pause rule).
- Focus on practicing them consistently for 30 days before adding additional habits.

Key Takeaways for Transformation

- **Freedom over Income**: Financial wealth matters most when it buys you time and personal freedom.
- **Purpose and Impact**: Wealth gains meaning when it aligns with your deeper values and creates significance beyond yourself.
- **Consistent Daily Habits**: Small, consistent actions build true wealth more effectively than occasional big moves.

Next Steps in the Book

- Learn advanced strategies for scaling and sustaining the wealthy entrepreneur lifestyle.
- Explore tools to align your wealth systems with your long-term purpose and legacy.
- Discover how to maintain balance between fulfillment today and financial security tomorrow.

By living as a wealthy entrepreneur, you'll transform your business success into a life of freedom, purpose, and impact.

Conclusion

The Integrated Wealth Journey

You now hold in your hands the complete Wealth Creation Method. This isn't just another business strategy or investment approach. It's a comprehensive system, a method that transforms your entrepreneurial success into a lasting personal fortune. In this book, we have meticulously constructed each component of this method: the Wealthy Entrepreneur's Flywheel, which generates sustainable profits; the Tax Reduction Code, which conserves your money; and the Personal Wealth Engine, which transforms these profits into enduring financial freedom.

Most entrepreneurs never make this critical connection. They build successful businesses but fail to create personal wealth that exists outside their companies. They work for decades and make good money, but they end up with surprisingly little to show for it. Their financial security remains tied to their continued work rather than assets they control.

This discrepancy arises due to the distinct nature of business profit and personal wealth, each of which has its own unique set of rules. True wealth comes from realizing that the income game and the wealth game are different.

Business success requires reinvestment, risk-taking, and constant attention. Wealth-building demands systematic extraction, protection, and patient compound growth. Without the bridge we've built in this book, these two worlds remain separate, creating the revenue trap that catches most entrepreneurs.

The Wealth Creation Method solves this problem by creating an integrated system through which your business success automatically fuels personal wealth-building. Your business becomes a wealth engine rather than just an income source. Your tax strategy supports both business growth and personal asset accumulation. Your investments grow independently of your work efforts. And your advisory team works together toward your wealth objectives rather than optimizing isolated pieces of your financial life.

This integrated approach creates results that far exceed what most entrepreneurs achieve. Instead of having a successful business but minimal personal assets, you build both simultaneously. Instead of facing retirement with anxiety despite decades of high income, you create a work-optional lifestyle with true financial security that exists outside your company. Instead of hoping for a business exit that may never materialize, you build wealth that provides freedom regardless of what happens with your business. You end up building a business you love that you could sell tomorrow but choose not to. You play the income game and the wealth game and win both!

From Knowledge to Transformation

Knowledge without action creates no results. The strategies in this book work only when you implement them consistently in your business and personal finances. The entrepreneurs who achieve remarkable wealth transformations aren't the ones who understand these concepts. They're the ones who apply them most consistently.

This implementation begins with your wealth habits. The Five-Minute Wealth Habit we explored creates the consistent actions that build fortune over time. This straightforward routine, which involves tracking your business and personal KPIs, verifying transfers, allocating wealth, identifying obstacles, and recognizing opportunities, serves as a bridge between understanding what to do and consistently executing it.

Beyond your habits, transformation requires systematic implementation of the core wealth strategies we've covered. The Wealth Transfer Protocol moves money consistently from business to personal accounts. The Tax Reduction Code minimizes the government's share of your success. The Personal Wealth Engine grows assets outside your business. And the Financial Ecosystem Integration Framework ensures that all these components work together seamlessly.

When these systems operate together, remarkable transformations occur. Within twelve months of proper implementation, you'll see measurable improvements in your personal balance sheet. Your Wealth Ratio will improve as assets outside your business grow faster than before. Your tax burden will decrease relative to your income. Your investment returns will increase through better asset allocation and tax efficiency. And your advisory team will identify opportunities worth tens or hundreds of thousands of dollars that were previously missed in your fragmented approach.

Within three to five years of consistent implementation, these improvements compound dramatically. Many entrepreneurs reach their Wealth Freedom Number decades earlier than they initially believed possible. They achieve this not by working harder or taking greater risks, but by systematically implementing the strategies we've covered. The difference between entrepreneurs who build significant wealth and those who merely earn good incomes isn't talent or luck—it's the consistent application of these wealth principles.

The most powerful transformation happens in your relationship with money and work. When you build wealth outside your business, you gain the freedom to make business decisions based on purpose rather than necessity. You can pursue opportunities because they excite you, not because you need the money. You can walk away from toxic clients or partners because your financial security doesn't depend on any single relationship. This psychological freedom creates both better business results and greater life satisfaction.

I've seen this transformation countless times. Entrepreneurs and founders who implemented these strategies built significant wealth and rediscovered their passion for business once financial pressure decreased. They made better strategic decisions because fear no longer clouded their judgment. They pursued more meaningful opportunities because necessity no longer dictated their choices. Their businesses performed better once wealth-building created the freedom to focus on purpose rather than just revenue and profit.

Your Wealth Creation Road Map

Your journey from revenue to wealth begins with immediate action. Not someday in the future when business conditions are perfect, but tomorrow morning with the first implementation of your Five-Minute Monthly

Wealth Habit. This simple routine creates the foundation for all other wealth strategies by maintaining awareness and consistency regardless of business chaos.

Within this first week, complete your Wealth Creation Assessment from Chapter 1. Calculate your current Wealth Ratio, Wealth Freedom Number, and Wealth Efficiency Score. These baseline measurements reveal exactly where you stand on the journey from business success to personal fortune. They show what's possible given your business performance and how much wealth-building potential you're currently capturing.

Within thirty days, schedule your first advisory team alignment meeting using the framework from Chapter 6. Bring together your key financial professionals to keep everyone working toward your wealth objectives rather than optimizing isolated pieces of your financial life. This initial meeting often identifies immediate opportunities worth tens of thousands of dollars that have been missed in your fragmented approach.

Within the next month, build your profit distribution system using the strategies from Chapter 3. Determine your optimal distribution percentage, establish your distribution timing framework, create your distribution pathway, implement distribution automation, and develop distribution protection rules. This systematic approach moves money consistently from business profit to personal wealth vehicles rather than being reinvested by default or absorbed by lifestyle expansion.

With these foundations in place, follow your personalized Wealth Timeline with quarterly check-ins to ensure that you're making proper progress. Review your Wealth Ratio improvement, Wealth Freedom Number progress, tax efficiency metrics, and investment performance at these regular intervals. These quarterly reviews create accountability and allow course corrections before small gaps become major setbacks.

As your wealth journey progresses, implement more advanced strategies based on your current phase—Survival, Stability, or Significance. The strategies appropriate for early-stage entrepreneurs differ dramatically from those most effective for established business owners approaching financial independence. Matching your wealth strategies to your current phase accelerates progress by focusing your limited time and attention on the approaches most relevant to your situation.

Keep in mind that wealth-building is not about accumulating wealth quickly. It's about getting wealthy systematically by harnessing the profit-generating power of your business to build assets you control. It's about creating financial security that exists independent of your company's performance. It's about transforming business success into personal fortune through deliberate, consistently applied strategies.

The path from profit to wealth isn't always easy. You'll face business challenges, market fluctuations, and competing priorities that test your commitment to wealth-building. During these inevitable challenges, return to the principles and strategies in this book. They provide the road map that keeps your wealth journey on track regardless of temporary obstacles or distractions.

Your entrepreneurial journey has already created business success. Now it's time to ensure that success translates into lasting personal fortune. This is for your personal benefit and for the security of your family, the impact you can create through strategic giving, and the legacy you will leave for future generations. The Wealth Creation Method provides the missing link between making money in your business and building wealth that creates true freedom, flexibility, and significance.

The journey begins now. The journey begins not with drastic changes or complex strategies, but with the simple habits and systematic approaches we've explored throughout this book.

You've built a successful business through talent, hard work, and perseverance. Now it's time to make sure success creates lasting financial freedom. The strategies in this book provide the missing manual for turning business success into personal fortune. Implement these steps consistently, and you'll join a select group of entrepreneurs, founders, and business owners who achieve TruWealth in all its dimensions—financial security, time freedom, and meaningful impact that extends far beyond your business achievements.

Here's What To Do Next

It's much more than a book!

Whenever you are ready, here are four ways we can help you take the next step on your journey to financial freedom.

1. Access All Your Free Bonuses

   By reading this book and saying yes to yourself, you have unlocked every bonus and resource in this book.

   Visit www.truwealthadvisors.com/book-resources to get all the resources mentioned in this book for free.

2. Schedule A Complimentary Wealth Creation Consultation

   If you found this book helpful and want some help getting pointed in the right direction, I'd love to invite you to chat with me and our team.

   Visit http://www.truwealthadvisors.com/strategycall to schedule a call with our team to discuss your action plan.

3. Hire Phil To Speak

   If you are looking for a dynamic speaker for your conference, event or mastermind, get in touch!

4. Connect on Social Media

   Let's keep the convo going! The journey doesn't end here. I'd love to connect with you on all social platforms.

   You can find us on social at @truwealthadvisors

Acknowledgments

This book would not have been possible without the incredible support, guidance, and inspiration of so many people.

To **Trish Calandra**, my wife and best friend—your love and belief in me have been the foundation of everything I've achieved. Thank you for always being by my side and inspiring me to be my best. I couldn't have done this without you.

To **Chris Harder** and **Lori Harder**, your mentorship and example have shaped not only our business but also our lives. Thank you for showing me what's possible when purpose meets action.

To **Jake Kelfer**, my publisher and friend. Your brilliance and dedication to helping others tell their story and succeed have been a guiding light. Thank you for your wisdom and encouragement.

To my **Elite Entrepreneur Mastermind family**, you've challenged me to think bigger, dream bolder, and step into my fullest potential. Your community has been a source of strength and inspiration.

This book is as much yours as it is mine. Thank you all for your belief in this mission and for walking alongside me on this journey. I am forever grateful.

About The Author

Phil Calandra is a distinguished business consultant, financial strategist, and entrepreneur dedicated to helping others achieve financial success and build lasting wealth. He has over thirty years of experience in financial services and business development. He has worked in the boardrooms of Fortune 500 giants such as Coca-Cola, Walt Disney Co., UPS, and Georgia-Pacific, as well as around the kitchen table and on Main Street USA with small business owners and founders, who have always been a passion. He has continuously refined his skills in business optimization and strategic planning.

Phil and his wife, Trish Calandra, built a successful insurance brokerage and registered investment advisory firm, which they scaled and exited in 2021. Their entrepreneurial journey reflects a deep commitment to providing transformative financial solutions for individuals and businesses alike.

Phil's thought leadership has been featured in *The Wall Street Journal*, *Forbes*, *Kiplinger Magazine*, and *The Atlanta Journal-Constitution*, cementing his reputation as an authority in financial strategy and wealth management. He also hosted an Atlanta-based personal finance radio show for nine years and a TV show for three years, where he shared his insights with a wide audience.

An accomplished athlete, Phil has completed three Ironman triathlons, twelve Ironman 70.3 triathlons, and nine marathons. He brings the same discipline, determination, and focus from his athletic pursuits to his professional life. In his free time, Phil enjoys snow skiing, cycling, and diving into a good book.

Phil is married to his business partner and best friend, Trish Calandra, and together they are still inspiring others with their shared passion for leadership, innovation, and living life to the fullest.

Made in the USA
Monee, IL
02 October 2026

62825079R10138